crochet
kid stuff
20 fun projects

crochet kid stuff
20 fun projects

Sharon Mann and Phyllis Sandford

Creative Publishing
international

acknowledgments

Special thanks to Kathleen Sams and Vicki Blizzard at Coats and Clark, Jane Garrison at YLI Corporation, Nick Greco at Yummy Yarns, and Kreinik Manufacturing Company, Inc. for contributing yarn and supporting our design efforts for this book.

To my best friend and husband Gary. I live my dream everyday, knee deep in yarn and my hands creating. Thanks, Gary, for taking such good care of me!
Sharon

I would like to dedicate the book to my wonderful husband Robert, for all his understanding while putting this book together.
Love you always.
Phyllis

Copyright 2007
Creative Publishing international
18705 Lake Drive East
Chanhassen, Minnesota 55317
1-800-328-3895
www.creativepub.com
All rights reserved

President/CEO: Ken Fund
Executive Managing Editor: Barbara Harold
Senior Editor: Linda Neubauer
Photo Stylist: Joanne Wawra
Creative Director: Michele Lanci-Altomare
Photo Art Director: Mary Rohl
Photographer: Steve Galvin
Production Manager: Linda Halls
Cover and Book Design: Mary Rohl
Page Layout Design: Danielle Smith

Library of Congress Cataloging-in-Publication Data
Mann, Sharon.
  Crochet kid stuff : 20 fun projects / Sharon Mann, Phyllis Sandford.
    p. cm.
  ISBN-13: 978-1-58923-295-2 (soft cover)
  ISBN-10: 1-58923-295-X (soft cover)
  1. Crocheting--Patterns. 2. Children's clothing. I. Sandford, Phyllis, 1943- II. Creative Publishing International. III. Title.
  TT825.M1723 2007
  746.43'4041--dc22   2006034242

Printed in China
10 9 8 7 6 5 4 3 2 1

Due to differing conditions, materials, and skill levels, the publisher and various manufacturers disclaim any liability for unsatisfactory results or injury due to improper use of tools, materials, or information in this book.

All rights reserved. No part of this work covered by the copyrights hereon may be reproduced or used in any form or by any means—graphic, electronic, or mechanical, including photocopying, recording, taping of information on storage and retrieval systems—without the written permission of the publisher.

contents

about the projects 6

for girls
glam sweater and scarf 10
headband and flower pin 14
shoestring backpack 16
shoestring summer hat 20
sideways sweater 24
cold floor slipper socks 26
chunky hat and scarf 30
so soft mittens 32
jelly yarn purse 36

for guys
color-stripe beanie 40
raglan crewneck sweater 44
fingerless gloves 50
striped hoodie 54
visor beanie 62
polo sweater 66

for fun
backpack dangles 76
fun and crazy pencil toppers 80
small change pouches 86
hacky sacks 88
snuggle-up blanket 90

crochet stitches 92
abbreviations 96

about the projects

Crocheting gifts for kids is a great way to express your love. Each stitch is a reminder of how much you care for them. Kids may not understand your need to give them handmade gifts, but someday the crocheted sweater, hat, or toy will have made a difference in their lives. They will remember and appreciate how you took the time to make them something special.

We are passing on our love for crochet to you. As children, we watched and learned from our grandmothers, mothers, and aunts (and sometimes grandfathers, fathers, and uncles) as they stitched, crocheted, and knitted for our families. It is thrilling to start with a ball of yarn, a crochet hook, and a pattern and end up with a beautiful garment. We hope you can pass on this loving tradition to a special child in your life.

The patterns in this book are easy and quick to make. We've used only basic stitches to eliminate frustration and provide a sense of mastery at the end of each project. Many of the patterns are easy enough for kids and other beginners who want to learn how to crochet.

We've included a wide variety of projects to keep your creative juices flowing. After you've made a few patterns, expand on the designs and develop your own creations. Make up your own animals using the backpack-dangle pattern, or design a new character with the simple pencil-topper pattern. We're sure your children will have some great ideas, too. The girls can create their own headband and flower designs. Boys may want to crochet an entire collection of hacky sacks.

The yarns we chose for each project can be substituted with yarns of equal weight and your own color preference. Just be sure to check your gauge when making clothes or accessories that need to fit. Thumb through the pages of this book and find some projects that intrigue you. Then head to the local craft store or yarn shop and have fun picking yarns. We think it's a sure bet you'll find a new passion with a ball of yarn and a simple crochet hook.

about the authors

Sharon Mann's passion is designing creative crochet projects. She has been published in books, magazines, and on the Internet. Other artistic endeavors include knitting, embellishment beading, needle felting, and fiber-art design. Check out her work and interests on her Web site: www.sharonmanndesigns.com.

Phyllis Sandford is a freelance designer and author. She has had a number of magazine articles and books published and has also created project sheets for manufacturers of craft materials. Her other interests include knitting, needle felting, felting, and decorative painting.

about the projects

for girls

8

crochet kid stuff

for girls

design by Phyllis Sandford

crochet kid stuff

glam sweater
and scarf

Ribbon-yarn ruffles at the bottom and accent edging around the neckline and sleeves add a bit of glamour to this cuddly-soft sweater. Easily made using only single, double, and triple crochet stitches, this sweater is sure to become a favorite for those cool, autumn, back-to-school days. For added warmth and stylish flair, crochet a matching scarf.

yarn
Lightweight smooth yarn
Shown: Microspun by Lion Brand, 100% microfiber acrylic, 2.50 oz (70 g)/168 yd (154 m): Buttercup, 3 skeins

Bulky-weight ribbon yarn
Shown: Incredible by Lion Brand, 100% nylon, 1.75 oz (50 g)/110 yd (100 m): City Lights, 1 skein

hooks
9/I (5.5 mm)
10½/K (6.5 mm)

stitches used
Single crochet
Single crochet through front loop
Double crochet
Double crochet through back loop
Triple crochet

gauge
4 stitches = 1" (2.5 cm) using 9/I hook

notion
Tapestry needle

finished size
6/7 (8/10, 12)

Alternating rows of single crochet through the front loop and double crochet through the back loop form the body and sleeves.

Front

Foundation row: Using 9/I (5.5 mm) hook and smooth yarn, ch 45 (49, 51). Work 1 dc in third ch from hook, 1 dc in each ch across, ch 1, turn.

Row 1: Work 1 sc tfl of each st across, ch 2, turn.

Row 2: Work 1 dc tbl of each st across, ch 1, turn.

Rep rows 1 and 2 until front is 15" (17", 18") [38.1 (43.2, 45.7) cm], fasten off.

Back

Work same as front.

Sleeves

Make 2.

Foundation row: Using 9/I (5.5 mm) hook and smooth yarn, ch 35 (39, 39). Work 1 dc in third ch from hook, 1 dc in each ch across, ch 1, turn.

Row 1: Work 1 sc tfl of each st across, ch 2, turn.

Row 2: Work 1 dc tbl of each st across, ch 1, turn.

Rep rows 1 and 2 until sleeve is 10" (12", 12") [25.4 (30.5, 30.5) cm], fasten off.

Construction

1. Sew front to back at shoulders, leaving center neck open 8" (8", 9") [20.3 (20.3, 22.9) cm].

2. Sew sleeves to sweater, matching upper center of each sleeve to shoulder seam.

3. Sew each side and underarm sleeve together in continuous seam.

Ribbon Borders

Lower edge

Rnd 1: Using ribbon yarn, working from RS, join yarn at bottom right seam. Ch 1, work 1 sc in same ch-1 sp, * 1 sc in next st, rep from * around, Sl st to first st.

Rnd 2: Ch 4, work 1 tr in next st, * ch 1, 2 tr in next st, rep from * around, Sl st to top of ch 4, fasten off.

Neck

Rnd 1: Join ribbon yarn to neck. Ch 1, work 1 sc in ch-1 sp, 1 sc in each st around.

Rnd 2: Work 2 sc in beg sc, 2 sc in each st around, Sl st to join, fasten off.

Sleeves

Rnd 1: Join ribbon yarn to sleeve bottom. Ch 1, work 1 sc in ch-1 sp, 1 sc in each st around, Sl st to join, fasten off.

Rep for other sleeve. Weave in all loose ends, using tapestry needle.

Scarf

Foundation row: Using 10 1/2/K (6.5 mm) hook and smooth yarn, ch 13. Work 1 dc in third ch from hook, 1 dc in each ch across, ch 1, turn—11 sts.

Row 1: Work 1 sc tfl of each st across, ch 2, turn.

Row 2: Work 1 dc tbl of each st across, ch 1, turn.

Rep rows 1 and 2 until scarf is 36" (91.4 cm) or desired length.

Using 9/I (5.5 mm) hook, join yarn at one corner and sc evenly along side to give scarf finished edge, fasten off. Rep on other side of scarf, fasten off.

Weave in loose ends, using tapestry needle.

Fringe

Cut 20 lengths of ribbon yarn, each 8" (20.3 cm) long. Fold ribbon in half and slip loop through first sp bet dc posts at one end of scarf. Bring ends of ribbon through loop and snug knot up to edge of scarf. Rep in each sp across both ends.

design by Phyllis Sandford

crochet kid stuff

headband
and flower pin

Crochet a sweet headband to match each of her sweaters. The flower pin on this one is detachable, so she can wear it on her jean jacket.

Headband

Foundation row: Make ch the length of headband. Work 1 dc in third ch from hook, 1 dc in each ch across, ch 1, turn.

Row 1: Work 1 sc tbl of each st across, ch 2, turn.

Row 2: Work 1 dc in each st across, ch 1, turn.

Row 3: Sc sides tog, forming tube, fasten off.

Slip headband through tube and sew ends. Weave in loose ends, using tapestry needle.

Flower

Foundation ring: Ch 10, Sl st to form ring.

Rnd 1: Ch 1, 10 sc in ring, Sl st to first sc.

Rnd 2: * Ch 10, sk 2 sc, sc in next sc * rep 4 times more, Sl st into bottom of ch 10—5 lps.

Rnd 3: [Sc, 2dc, 2 tr, 2dc, sc] in each loop, Sl st in first sc.

Bobble: Ch 3, * yo, insert hook into third ch from hook, yo draw through 2 lps * rep 3 times in same st, yo, draw through all loops on hook, Sl st to opposite side of flower ring, fasten off.

Finishing

1. Using beading thread and beading needle, sew beads to every other stitch along both sides of headband. Sew beads randomly to flower.

2. Stitch pin back to back of flower. Pin flower to headband.

yarn
Lightweight cotton, novelty, or acrylic yarn
Shown: Microspun by Lion Brand, 100% microfiber acrylic, 2.50 oz (70 g)/168 yd (154 m): Buttercup, 1 skein

hook
4/E (3.5 mm)

stitches used
Single crochet
Single crochet through back loop
Double crochet
Triple crochet
Bobble

gauge
4 sts = 1" (2.5 cm)

notions
Headband
Sewing needle
Sewing thread to match yarn
Tapestry needle
Beads
Beading thread
Beading needle
Pin back

design by Phyllis Sandford

crochet kid stuff

shoestring backpack

Your girl will be ready for anything with her shoestring backpack. This fun ribbon yarn looks like shoe laces but it comes in a continuous length. Made from acrylic, it's totally washable and durable. With basic stitches and an easy design, you can whip up this handy carry-all in no time. Adjust the strap length to suit her, and she will carry it comfortably wherever she goes.

yarn
Super bulky ribbon yarn
Shown: Shoelace by YLI, 100% acrylic, 5.8 oz (165 g)/100 yd (90 m): Sky Blue #007 (A), 1 skein; White/Sky Blue Wave #W07 (B), 1 skein

hook
P (11.5 mm)

stitches used
Single crochet
Double crochet

gauge
1½ sts = 1" (2.5 cm)

notions
Stitch marker
Tapestry needle
Sewing needle
Sewing thread

finished size
9" wide × 14" tall
(22.9 × 35.6 cm)
24" (61 cm) circumference

Super bulky ribbon yarn is worked in rounds of single crochet.

Backpack

Foundation rnd: With A, ch 4, Sl st in first ch to form ring. Work 6 sc in ring, pm at beg of rnds, do not join after each rnd unless instructed to do so.

Rnd 1: Work 2 sc in each sc around—12 sc.

Rnd 2: * Work 1 sc, 2 sc in next sc, rep from * 5 times more—18 sc.

Rnd 3: * Work 2 sc, 2 sc in next sc, rep from * 5 times more—24 sc.

Rnd 4: * Work 3 sc, 2 sc in next sc, rep from * 5 times more—30 sc.

Rnd 5: * Work 4 sc, 2 sc in next sc, rep from * 5 times more—36 sc.

Rnd 6: Work 1 sc in each sc around—36 sc.

Rnds 7–12: With B, work 1 sc in each sc around—36 sc.

Rnds 13–18: With A, work 1 sc in each sc around—36 sc.

Rnds 19–22: With B, work 1 sc in each sc around—36 sc.

Rnds 23–24: With A, work 1 sc in each sc around—36 sc.

Rnd 25: Cont with A, * work [1 sc, 2 dc, 1 sc] in first sc, Sl st in next sc, rep from * around, fasten off.

Weave in loose ends, using tapestry needle.

Drawstring

Using 1 strand of each color held tog, ch for 48" (121.9 cm) or desired length, fasten off. Tie knot at each end of drawstring. Weave drawstring in and out of sc sts below ruffle. Pull tight to cinch backpack. Tie in loose knot or bow for closure.

Straps

Make 2.

Foundation row: With either color, ch 5. Work 1 sc in second ch from hook, 1 sc in each ch across, ch 1, turn.

Row 1: Work 1 sc in each sc across, ch 1, turn—4 sc.

Rep row 1 for 24 rows more, fasten off. Weave in loose ends, using tapestry needle.

Using tapestry needle and ribbon yarn, sew top of straps to top of bag just below ruffle, 4" (10.2 cm) apart. Sew bottom of straps to bottom of bag, 3" (7.6 cm) apart.

Clusters of single crochet, double crochet, single crochet, worked in every other stitch, form a short ruffle at the upper edge of the backpack.

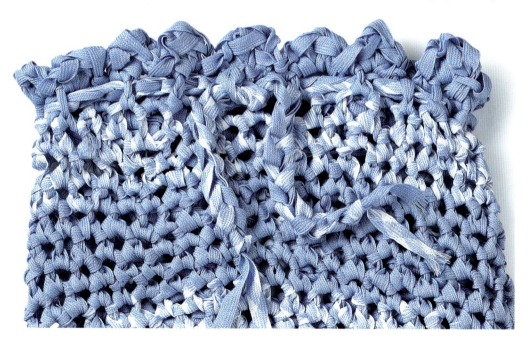

design by Phyllis Sandford

crochet kid stuff

shoestring summer hat

Crochet a quick-and-easy summer hat with shoelace ribbon yarn to match the backpack on page 16. It's lightweight and airy—just enough there to shade her head from the sun. For a bit of sassy style, turn up the brim and add a crocheted flower. It's totally washable and packable and will mold to her head each time she puts it on. What could be more fun?

yarn
Super bulky ribbon yarn
Shown: Shoelace by YLI, 100% acrylic, 5.8 oz (165 g)/100 yd (90 m): Sky Blue #007 (A), 1 skein; White/Sky Blue Wave #W07 (B), 1 skein

hook
P (11.5 mm)

stitches used
Single crochet
Double crochet

gauge
1½ sts = 1" (2.5 cm)

notions
Stitch marker
Tapestry needle
Pin back
Sewing needle
Sewing thread

finished size
Small: 20" (50.8 cm) circumference, 6" (15.2 cm) top to brim
Medium: 22" (55.9 cm) circumference, 6½" (16.5 cm) top to brim

Hat is worked in rounds of single crochet stitches, beginning at the center of the crown.

Hat
Small or medium
Foundation rnd: With A, ch 4, Sl st in first ch to form ring. Work 6 sc in ring, pm at beg of rnds, do not join after each rnd unless instructed to do so.

Small
Rnd 1: With A, work 2 sc in each sc around—12 sc.

Rnd 2: * Work 1 sc, 2 sc in next sc, rep from * 5 times more—18 sc.

Rnd 3: * Work 2 sc, 2 sc in next sc, rep from * 5 times more—24 sc.

Rnds 4–7: With B, work 1 sc in each sc around.

Rnds 8–11: With A, work 1 sc in each sc around.

Rnds 12–14: With B, work 1 sc in each sc around.

Rnds 15–16: With A, work 1 sc in each sc around.

Rnd 17: Cont with A, * Sl st in next sc, work [1 sc, 2 dc, 1 sc] in next sc, rep from * around, Sl st in first sc, fasten off.

Weave in loose ends, using tapestry needle.

Medium:
Rnd 1: With A, work 2 sc in each sc around—12 sc.

Rnd 2: * Work 1 sc, 2 sc in next sc, rep from * 5 times more—18 sc.

Rnd 3: * Work 2 sc, 2 sc in next sc, rep from * 5 times more—24 sc.

Rnd 4: * Work 3 sc, 2 sc in next sc, rep from * 5 times more—30 sc.

Rnds 5–7: With B, work 1 sc in each sc around.

Rnds 8–11: With A, work 1 sc in each sc around.

Rnds 12–14: With B, work 1 sc in each sc around.

Rnds 15–16: With A, work 1 sc in each sc around.

Rnd 17: Cont with A, * Sl st in next sc, * work [1 sc, 2 dc, 1 sc] in next sc, rep from * around, Sl st in first sc, fasten off.

Weave in loose ends, using tapestry needle.

Flower

Foundation rnd: With A, ch 4, Sl st in first ch to form ring. Work 10 sc in ring, Sl st to first ch.

Rnd 1: * Ch 4, sk 1 sc, sc in next st, rep from * 4 times more (5 lps), fasten off.

Rnd 2: Join B to sp bet 2 lps, * work [1 sc, 2 dc, 1 sc] in sp bet lps, rep from * 4 times more, Sl st to first sc, fasten off.

Weave in loose ends, using tapestry needle.

Sew on pin back and attach flower to hat.

Crocheted flower has a pin backing so it can be removed from the hat and worn on a jacket.

design by Phyllis Sandford

crochet kid stuff

sideways sweater

Crochet this cute short-sleeved sweater in a weekend. It can be worn over a T-shirt or turtleneck or by itself.

Sweater Front and Back
Make 2.

Sweater is crocheted side to side. Measure your child's chest size before starting. You can inc or dec rows on back and front if necessary, keeping an even row count.

Foundation row: Ch 34 (36, 38, 40). Work 1 dc in third ch from hook, 1 dc in each ch across, ch 2, turn—32 (34, 36, 38) sts.

Row 1: Starting with first st, * work 4 dc tbl, 4 dc tfl, rep from * 4 times more, 4 dc tbl, ch 2, turn.

Row 2: Rep row 1 for 20 (22, 24, 26) times more—22 (24, 26, 28) rows—fasten off.

Sleeves
Make 2.

Foundation row: Ch 34 (36, 38, 40). Work 1 dc in third ch from hook, 1 dc in each ch across, ch 2, turn—32 (34, 36, 38) sts.

Row 1: Starting with first st, * work 4 dc tbl, 4 dc tfl, rep from * 4 times more, 4 dc tbl, ch 2, turn.

Row 2: Rep row 1 for 5 (7, 7, 9) times more—7 (9, 9, 11) rows—fasten off.

Construction

1. Turn front and back of sweater vertically, and sew shoulder seams together, using tapestry needle.

2. Fold each sleeve in half, RS out, and align with center of shoulder seam. Sew each sleeve to sweater.

3. Sew sleeve and sweater side seams.

4. Weave in loose ends.

yarn
Bulky-weight slubbed yarn
Shown: Tessin by Muench, 22% cotton/35% acrylic/43% wool, 3.5 oz (100 g)/110 yd (100 m): Green #65806, 5 skeins

hook
10½/K (6.5 mm)

stitches used
Double crochet
Double crochet through front loop
Double crochet through back loop

gauge
1½ sts = 1" (2.5 cm)

notion
Tapestry needle

finished size
(front and back sizes)
Size 6: 15" × 10½" (38.1 × 26.9 cm)
Size 8: 16" × 12½" (40.6 × 31.8 cm)
Size 10: 17" × 14" (43.2 × 35.6 cm)
Size 12: 18" × 15" (45.7 × 38.1 cm)

design by Phyllis Sandford

crochet kid stuff

cold floor slipper socks

When the temperature dips into the single digits, these bright and cozy slipper socks will keep your child's feet warm and toasty. Two yarns held together throughout give the slippers extra body and fun texture. Follow the directions on the yarn label for laundering them.

yarn
Lightweight bouclé yarn
Shown: Mystery by Artful Yarns, 40% wool/25% cotton/20% acrylic/15% nylon, 1.8 oz (50 g)/98 yd (88 m): color #4, 2 skeins

Bulky-weight smooth yarn
Shown: Encore Chunky by Plymouth, 75% acrylic/25% wool, 3.5 oz (100 g)/143 yd (132 m): color #137, 2 skeins

hook
6/G (4 mm)
or
8/H (5 mm)

stitches used
Single crochet
Single crochet through back loop

gauge
3 sts = 1" (2.5 cm) on 8/H hook
4 sts = 1" (2.5 cm) on 6/G hook

notions
Tapestry needle
Stitch marker

finished size
Small: 8½" (21.6 cm) heel to toe
Medium: 9" (24.1 cm) heel to toe

Crocheting through the back loop of the stitches creates ribbed texture.

Slipper Socks

Make 2.
For size small, use 6/G (4 mm) hook. For size medium, use 8/H (5 mm) hook. Use one strand of each yarn held tog.

Beg with ribbing
Foundation row: Ch 13, work 1 sc in second ch from hook, 1 sc in each ch across, ch 1, turn.

Row 1: Work 1 sc in first st, 1 sc tbl of each st across, ch 1, turn.

Rep row 1 for 24 rows more, fasten off, leaving an 8" (20.3 cm) tail. Sew ends tog to form tube. Weave in loose ends, using tapestry needle.

Sock top
Rnd 1: Join yarn to either side of cuff, sc 31 sts evenly around, pm for beg of rnd, and cont in rnds.

Rnds 2–8: Work 1 sc tbl of each st around—31 sts.

Heel flap
Rows 1–9: Ch 1, work 12 sc tbl across, ch 1, turn.

Turn heel
WS facing you, work 12 sc tbl across flap. RS facing you, fold flap in half (inward), bring bottom of flap up, Sl st in right-hand corner, work 19 sc tbl across front of sock, Sl st flap to left-hand corner of sock, and cont with 12 sc tbl across flap. Place marker for beg of rnd (right-hand corner) and cont rnds—31 sts.

Foot
Rnd 1: Work 31 sc tbl around.

Rnd 2: Work 2 sc tbl of first st, at corner of sock, 18 sc tbl across front, 2 sc tbl of next st, 11 sc tbl across—33 sts.

Rnd 3: Work 2 sc tbl of first st, 19 sc tbl across front, 2 sc tbl of next st, 12 sc tbl across—35 sts.

Rnd 4–8: Work 35 sc tbl around (add or dec rows, depending on length of your child's foot).

Toe
Rnd 9: Sk st at corner of sock, work 20 sc tbl across, sk st at corner of sock, 13 sc tbl across—33 sts.

Rnd 10: Sk st, work 19 sc tbl across, sk st, 12 sc tbl across—31 sts.

Rnd 11: Sk st, work 18 sc tbl across, sk st, 11 sc tbl across—29 sts.

Rnd 12: Sk st, work 17 sc tbl across, sk st, 10 sc tbl across—27 sts.

Rnd 13: Sk st, work 16 sc tbl across, sk st, 9 sc tbl across—25 sts.

Rnd 14: Sk st, work 15 sc tbl across, sk st, 8 sc tbl across—23 sts.

Rnd 15: Sk st, work 14 sc tbl across, sk st, 7 sc tbl across—21 sts.

Rnd 16: Work 21 sc tbl around.

Rnd 17: Work 21 sc tbl around, fasten off, leaving 10" (25.4 cm) tail. Turn sock inside out and, using tapestry needle, weave yarn in and out of sts, pulling tight.

Sew sides of heels tog, using tapestry needle. Weave in loose ends.

Cuff is worked flat vertically, then sewn together. Slipper is then joined to the cuff and worked in rounds to the heel flap and from the heel flap to the toe.

cold floor slipper socks

design by Phyllis Sandford

crochet kid stuff

chunky hat and scarf

This matching hat and scarf are so easy to make, you can use this project to teach a child to crochet. Both pieces are made entirely with single crochet worked through the back loop. The hat is a flat rectangle sewn up and gathered at the top.

Scarf

Foundation row: Ch 8. Work 1 sc in second ch from hook, 1 sc in each ch across, ch 1, turn—7 sts.

Row 1: Work 1 sc tbl of first st, 1 sc tbl of each st across, ch 1, turn.

Rep row 1 until you have only 3 yd (2.7 m) of first skein left, fasten off. Weave in loose ends, using tapestry needle.

Fringe

Using rem 3 yd (2.7 m) of yarn, cut 14 lengths of yarn, each 7" (17.8 cm) long for fringe. Tie seven fringe pieces at each end of scarf with Larks Head Knot (fold yarn in half, pull bet sc posts, bring ends of yarn through lp, pull tight).

Hat

Foundation row: Ch 21 (23). Work 1 sc in second ch from hook, 1 sc in each ch across, ch 1, turn—20 (22) sts.

Row 1: Work 1 sc tbl of each st across, ch 1, turn.

Rep row 1 until hat is 7" (17.8 cm), fasten off.

Construction

1. Sew sides of hat together, forming tube.

2. Cut 18" (45.7 cm) piece of yarn and weave in and out loops at top of tube, pull yarn tightly to gather. Tie knot and weave in loose ends.

3. To make tassel, wind 1 yd (0.9 m) of yarn around a 3" × 5" (7.6 × 12.7 cm) piece of cardboard. Remove yarn and tie knot around middle of loops with 8" (20.3 cm) piece of yarn. Tie tassel to top of hat. Cut loops. Weave in loose ends.

yarn
Super-bulky multicolor smooth yarn
Shown: Jiffy Thick & Quick by Lion Brand, 100% acrylic, 5 oz (140 g)/ 84 yd (76 m):
Rocky Mountains #208, 2 skeins

hook
Q (16 mm)

stitches used
Single crochet
Single crochet through back loop

gauge
1 st = 1" (2.5 cm)

notions
Tapestry needle
3" × 5" (7.6 × 12.7 cm) piece of cardboard

finished size
Scarf: 4" × 45" (10.2 × 114.3 cm)
Hat (small): 7" (17.8 cm) from crown to rim; 20" (50.8 cm) circumference
Hat (medium): 7" (17.8 cm) from crown to rim; 22" (55.9 cm) circumference

design by Phyllis Sandford

mittens so soft

Keep those precious hands and fingers warm with easy-to-crochet mittens. Single crochet stitches help block out the cold. Combining a mohair-blend yarn with a lightweight, smooth, wool-blend yarn makes them so very soft, too. Make them in all her favorite colors.

yarn
Lightweight mohair yarn
Shown: Kidsilk Haze by Rowan, 70% kid mohair/30% silk, 0.9 oz (25 g)/229 yd (210 m): #598, 1 skein

Lightweight smooth yarn
Shown: Country Naturals by Cleckheaton, 85% wool/10% acrylic/5% viscose, 1.8 oz (50 g)/109 yd (100 m): #1832, 1 skein

hook
6/G (4 mm)
or
8/H (5 mm)

stitches used
Single crochet
Single crochet through back loop

gauge
4 sts = 1" (2.5 cm) using 6/G hook
3 sts = 1" (2.5 cm) using 8/H hook

notions
Tapestry needle
Stitch marker

finished size
Small: 9" (22.9 cm) cuff to top
Medium: 9½" (24.1 cm) cuff to top

Mittens

Make 2.

For size small, use 6/G (4 mm) hook. For size medium, use 8/H (5 mm) hook. Use one strand of each yarn held tog throughout.

Beg with cuff
Foundation row: Ch 13, work 1 sc in second ch from hook, 1 sc in each ch across, ch 1, turn—12 sts.

Row 1: Work 1 sc tbl of first st, 1 sc tbl of each st across, ch 1, turn.

Rep row 1 for 23 rows more, fasten off, leaving 8" (20.3 cm) tail. Sew ends tog to form tube. Weave in loose ends, using tapestry needle.

Beg palm
Rnd 1: Join yarn to either side of cuff and work 24 sc evenly around, pm for beg of rnd.

Rnds 2–4: Work 1 sc in each st around.

Rnd 5: Work 2 sc in first st, 1 sc in each of next 11 sts, 2 sc in next st, 1 sc in each of next 11 sts, ch 1, turn—26 sts.

Beg thumb opening, work in rows
Rows 6–10: Work 1 sc in first st, 1 sc in each st across, ch 1, turn.

Row 11: Work 1 sc in each st across, do not turn.

Rnd 12: Work 1 sc in next st to join rnd, 1 sc in each st around. Cont in rnds.

Rnds 13–15: Work 1 sc in each st around (lengthen or shorten by adding or dec rnds at this time).

Rnd 16: Sk first st (dec), work 1 sc in each of next 11 sts, sk st (dec), 1 sc in each st around—24 sts.

Rnd 17: Work 1 sc in each st around.

Rnd 18: Sk first st (dec), work 1 sc in each of next 10 sts, sk st (dec), 1 sc in each st around—22 sts.

Rnd 19: Work 1 sc in each st around.

Rnd 20: Sk first st (dec), work 1 sc in each of next 9 sts, sk st (dec), 1 sc in each st around—20 sts.

Rnd 21: Work 1 sc in each st around.

Rnd 22: Sk first st (dec), work 1 sc in each of next 8 sts, sk st (dec), 1 sc in each st around—18 sts.

Rnd 23: Work 1 sc in each st around.

Rnd 24: Sk first st (dec), work 1 sc in each of next 7 sts, sk st (dec), 1 sc in each st around—16 sts.

Rnd 25: Work 1 sc in each st around, Sl st in first st, leaving 10" (25.4 cm) tail. Weave yarn in and out of sc, using tapestry needle to close top of mitten. Fasten off. Weave in loose ends.

Thumb

Rnd 1: Join yarn and work 15 sc evenly around thumb opening, pm for beg of rnd.

Rnd 2: Work 1 sc in each of first 7 sts, sk st (dec), 1 sc in each of next 6 sts, sk st (dec).

Rnd 3: Work 1 sc in each of first 6 sts, sk st (dec), 1 sc in each of next 5 sts, sk st (dec).

Rnd 4: Work 1 sc in each of first 5 sts, sk st (dec), 1 sc in each of next 4 sts, sk st (dec).

Rnd 5: Work 1 sc in each of first 4 sts, sk st (dec), 1 sc in each of next 3 sts, sk st (dec).

Rnd 6: Work 1 sc in each st around (add another row if thumb needs to be longer).

Rnd 7: Work 1 sc in each st around, Sl st in last sc, leaving 5" (12.7 cm) tail. Weave yarn in and out of sc, using tapestry needle to close top of thumb. Fasten off. Weave in loose ends.

Cuff is worked flat vertically, then sewn together. Mitten is joined to cuff and worked in rounds to bottom of thumb opening; worked in rows through thumb opening; and then in rounds to top. Thumb is joined to opening and worked in rounds.

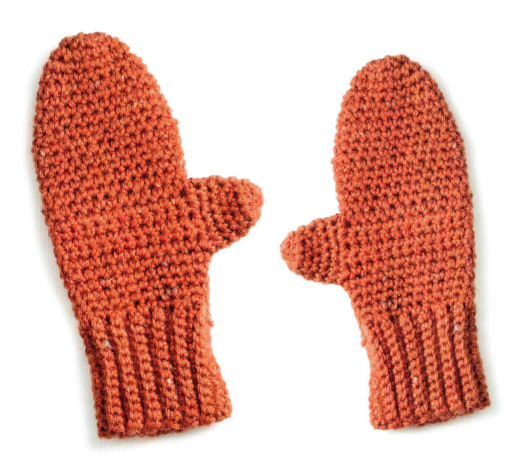

design by Phyllis Sandford

crochet kid stuff

jelly yarn purse

This unique purse is quick to make and fun to carry. Jelly yarn makes it perfect for a fashion-forward girl. In fact, she may want to make her own!

Purse

Use a steel hook with Jelly Yarn—this yarn will stick to a plastic hook and make it very difficult to crochet.

Foundation row: With A, ch 21. Work 1 dc in third ch from hook, 1 dc in each ch across, ch 2, turn—19 sts.

Row 1: Work 1 dc in first st, 1 dc in each st across, ch 2, turn.

Rep row 1 for 17 rows more, fasten off. Weave in ends, using tapestry needle.

Construction

1. Fold purse at seventh row. Join B at bottom of left-hand fold, sc sides together. Continue sc around top flap to right side, sc right-hand side of purse together, fasten off. Weave in loose ends.

2. Join C to flap and sc evenly around, fasten off. Weave in loose ends.

3. Sew button to purse front with matching thread. For closure, button will fit through dc spaces on flap.

Strap

Foundation row: With A, ch 46. Work 1 dc in third ch from hook, 1 dc in each ch across, ch 2, turn—44 sts.

Row 1: Work 1 dc in first st, 1 dc in each st across, fasten off. Weave in loose ends.

Join B 2" (5.1 cm) from one end of strap. Holding the strap end over the purse back, even with the side, sc around the strap end, catching the sts of the purse back in each st. At flap fold, cont sc in each st around strap to 2" (5.1 cm) from opposite end. Secure opposite end to other side of purse back in same manner. Cont sc in each st along remaining edge of strap, fasten off. Weave in loose ends.

yarn
Bulky-weight smooth vinyl yarn
Shown: Jelly Yarn by Yummy Yarns, 100% vinyl, 8.5 oz (240 g)/65 yd (60m): Lemon-Lime Ice (A), 1 skein; Hot Pink Candy (B), 1 skein

Bulky-weight fur/tape yarn
Shown: Moda Dea Fur Ever by Coats & Clark, 68% polyester/32% nylon, 1.76 oz (50 g)/49 yd (45 m): Limeade (C), 1 skein

hook
10½/K (6.5 mm) (use steel hook with Jelly Yarn)

stitches used
Single crochet
Double crochet

gauge
3 dc = 1" (2.5 cm)

notions
Tapestry needle
Button, 1" (2.5 cm) diameter
Sewing needle
Thread to match yarn

finished size
8" wide × 7" tall
(20.3 × 17.8 cm)

for guys

crochet kid stuff

design by Sharon Mann

crochet kid stuff

color-stripe beanie

Boys like the simplicity of this hat—no frills. Girls like beanies, too. When your kids are skateboarding, standing at the bus stop, meeting friends at the mall, or just hanging out at home, they'll be showing off their beanies to friends. Don't be surprised if the neighbor kids come knocking at your door for one!

yarn
Medium-weight smooth yarn
Shown: Red Heart Super Saver by Coats & Clark, 100% acrylic, 7 oz (198 g)/364 yd (333 m): Royal #0385 (A), 1 skein

Shown: Red Heart Kids by Coats & Clark, 100% acrylic, 4 oz (113 g)/242 yd (223 m): Crayon #2930 (B), 1 skein

hook
8/H (5 mm)

stitches used
Single crochet
Double crochet

gauge
4 sts = 1" (2.5 cm)

notions
Stitch marker
Tapestry needle

finished size
Small: 7¾" (19.7 cm) from crown to rim; 20" (50.8 cm) circumference
Medium: 8" (20.3 cm) from crown to rim; 21" (53.3 cm) circumference

When changing colors in the round, always end the previous row with a slip stitch at the end of the round and fasten off. Join the new color, chain 1, and follow the instructions. At the end of the first round of the new color, slip stitch into the ch 1 and continue the pattern. This method keeps the different color rounds even and minimizes a stair-step look to the stripe.

Beanie

Beanie is worked in rnds, starting at top.

Small

Foundation rnd: With A, ch 3, Sl st in first ch to form ring. Work 6 sc in ring, pm at beg of rnds, do not join after each rnd unless instructed to do so.

Rnd 1: Work 2 sc in each sc around—12 sc.

Rnd 2: * Work 1 sc, 2 sc in next sc, rep from * 5 times more—18 sc.

Rnd 3: * Work 2 sc, 2 sc in next sc, rep from * 5 times more—24 sc.

Rnd 4: * Work 3 sc, 2 sc in next sc, rep from * 5 times more—30 sc.

Rnd 5: * Work 4 sc, 2 sc in next sc, rep from * 5 times more—36 sc.

Rnd 6: * Work 5 sc, 2 sc in next sc, rep from * 5 times more—42 sc.

Rnd 7: * Work 6 sc, 2 sc in next sc, rep from * 5 times more—48 sc.

Rnd 8: * Work 7 sc, 2 sc in next sc, rep from * 5 times more—54 sc.

Rnd 9: * Work 8 sc, 2 sc in next sc, rep from * 5 times more—60 sc.

Rnd 10: * Work 9 sc, 2 sc in next sc, rep from * 5 times more—66 sc.

Rnd 11: * Work 10 sc, 2 sc in next sc, rep from * 5 times more—72 sc.

Rnds 12–18: Work 1 sc in each sc, do not join at beg—72 sc.

Rnd 19: Work 1 sc in each sc, Sl st in first sc, fasten off A.

Rnd 20: Join B, ch 1, work 1 sc in each sc, Sl st in first ch-sp.

Rnds 21–22: Ch 3, work 1 dc in each sc, Sl st in top of ch 3.

Rnd 23: Ch 1, work 1 sc in each dc, Sl st in first sc, fasten off B.

Rnd 24: Join A, ch 1, work 1 sc in each sc, do not join at beg.

Rnds 25–26: With A, rep rnd 24.

Rnd 27: Work 1 sc in each sc, Sl st in first sc, fasten off A.

Rnd 28: Join B, ch 3, work 1 dc in each sc, Sl st in top of ch 3.

Rnd 29: Work 1 sc each dc, do not join at beg, Sl st in first sc, fasten off.

Medium
Foll patt for size small until rnd 11.

Rnd 12: * Work 11 sc, 2 sc in next sc, rep from * 3 times evenly —76 sc.

Rnds 13–18: Work 1 sc in each sc, do not join at beg—76 sc.

Rnd 19: Work 1 sc in each sc, Sl st in first sc, fasten off A.

Rnd 20: Join B, ch 1, work 1 sc in each sc, Sl st in first ch-sp.

Rnds 21–22: Ch 3, work 1 dc in each sc, Sl st in top of ch 3.

Rnd 23: Ch 1, work 1 sc in each dc, Sl st in first sc, fasten off B.

Rnd 24: Join A, ch 1, work 1 sc in each sc, do not join at beg.

Rnds 25–26: With A, rep rnd 24.

Rnd 27: Work 1 sc in each sc, Sl st in first sc, fasten off A.

Rnd 28: Join B, ch 3, work 1 dc in each sc, Sl st in top of ch 3.

Rnds 29–30: Work 1 sc in each dc, do not join at beg, Sl st in first sc, fasten off.

Add or reduce sc rnds, bet rounds 24–27 if the hat length needs to be longer or shorter.

Weave in loose ends, using tapestry needle.

When changing colors, carry the first and second color along the back for a few stitches to avoid having to weave loose threads at the end.

crochet kid stuff

design by Sharon Mann

raglan crewneck sweater

This basic raglan crewneck sweater is made in one piece from the neck down to the underarm. Front, back, and sleeves are then added on separately and seamed together. Ribbings are made separately and sewn to the bottom of the sweater body and sleeves. You'll find it very easy to make, and it will become one of your child's favorites.

yarn
Lightweight smooth yarn
Shown: Red Heart TLC Essentials by Coats & Clark, 100% acrylic, 6 oz (170 g)/12 yd (285 m):Taupe #2335 (A), 3 (4, 4) skeins; Dark Brown #2368 (B), 1 skein

Shown: Red Heart Super Saver by Coats & Clark, 100% acrylic, 7 oz (198 g)/364 yd (333 m): Delft Blue #0885 (C), 1 skein

hook
9/I (5.5 mm)

stitches used
Single crochet
Single crochet through back loop
Double crochet
Double crochet through front loop
Double crochet through back loop

gauge
3 sc = 1" (2.5 cm)

notion
Tapestry needle

finished size
6/7 (8/10, 12)

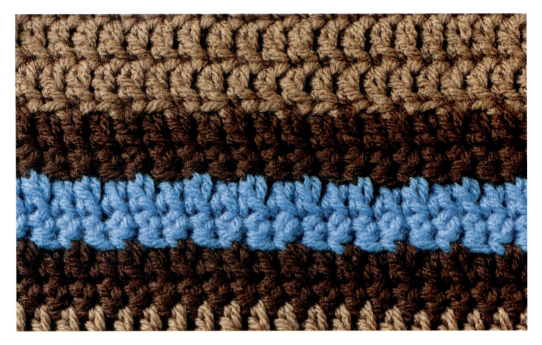

Alternating rows of single crochet and double crochet through the front and back loops form the body and sleeves of the sweater.

Front and Back Ribbing
Make 2.
To inc or dec chest size, rows can be added or dec at raglan neck. To inc length of sleeve, add rows before dec beg.

Foundation row: With A, ch 9. Work 1 sc in second ch from hook, 1 sc in each ch across, ch 1, turn.

Row 1: Work 1 sc in first st, 1 sc tbl of each st across, 1 sc in last st, ch 1, turn.

Rep row 1, 52 (56, 60) times more, fasten off—54 (58, 62) rows.

Sleeve Ribbing
Make 2.

Foundation row: With A, ch 9. Work 1 sc in second ch from hook, 1 sc in each ch across, ch 1, turn.

Row 1: Work 1 sc in first st, 1 sc tbl in each st across, 1 sc in last st, ch 1, turn.

Rep row 1, 22 (24, 26) times more, fasten off—24 (26, 28) rows.

Upper Body
Work from neck down.

Foundation rnd: With A, ch 71, work 1 sc in second ch from hook, 1 sc in each ch around, Sl st in first ch to form ring—70 sts.

Rnd 1: Ch 4, work 2 dc in first st, 19 dc, [2 dc, ch 1, 2 dc] in next st (corner), 14 dc, [2 dc, ch 1, 2 dc] in next st (corner), 19 dc, [2 dc, ch 1, 2 dc] in next st (corner), 14 dc, 1 dc in beg st, Sl st to third ch of ch 4, Sl st in next ch.

Rnd 2: Ch 4, work 2 dc in ch-1 sp, 23 dc, [2 dc, ch 1, 2 dc] in ch-1 sp (corner), 18 dc, [2 dc, ch 1, 2 dc] in ch-1 sp (corner), 24 dc, [2 dc, ch 1, 2 dc] in ch-1 sp (corner), 18 dc,

1 dc in beg ch-1 sp, Sl st to third ch of ch 4, Sl st in next ch.

Note: Sts per row inc on front, back, and shoulders with added sts in each corner.

Size 6/7: Rep row 2, 6 times more, fasten off. Front and back—52 sts. Shoulders—48 sts.

Size 8/10: Rep row 2, 7 times more, fasten off. Front and back—56 sts. Shoulders—50 sts.

Size 12: Rep row 2, 8 times more, fasten off. Front and back—60 sts. Shoulders—56 sts.

Front and Back
Row 1: With B, RS facing you, ch 3 (counts as dc) in right-hand ch-1 sp, * work 1 dc tbl of next st, 1 dc tfl of next st, rep from * across, 1 dc in ch-1 sp, ch 1, turn—54 (58, 62) sts.

Row 2: Work 1 sc in first st, 1 sc in each st across, ch 2, turn.

Row 3: With C, work 1 dc in first st, * 1 dc tbl of next st, 1 dc tfl of next st, rep from * across, 1 dc in last st, ch 1, turn.

Row 4: Work 1 sc in first st, 1 in each st across, ch 2, turn, fasten off C.

Row 5: With B, work 1 dc in first st, * 1 dc tbl of next st, 1 dc tfl of next st, rep from * across, 1 dc in last st, ch 1, turn.

Row 6: Work 1 sc in first st, 1 sc in each st across, ch 2, turn, fasten off B.

Row 7: With A, work 1 dc in first st, 1 dc in each st across, ch 1, turn.

Row 8: Work 1 sc in first st, 1 sc in each st across, ch 2, turn.

Size 6/7: Rep rows 6 and 7, 8 times more.

Size 8/10: Rep rows 6 and 7, 9 times more.

Size 12: Rep rows 6 and 7, 10 times more.

Last row: Work 1 sc in first st, 1 sc in each st across, fasten off.

Sew ribbing to bottom of front and back.

Sleeves
Row 1: With B, RS facing, ch 3 in right-hand ch-1 sp, * work 1 dc tbl of next st, 1 dc tfl of next st, rep from * across, 1 dc in ch-1 sp, ch 1, turn—50 (52, 56) sts.

Row 2: Work 1 sc in first st, 1 sc in each st across, ch 2, turn.

Row 3: With C, work 1 dc in first st, * 1 dc tbl of next st, 1 dc tfl of next st, rep from * across, 1 dc in last st, ch 1, turn.

Row 4: Work 1 sc in first st, 1 sc in each st across, ch 2, turn, fasten off C.

Row 5: With B, work 1 dc in first st, * 1 dc tbl of next st, 1 dc tfl of next st, rep from * across, 1 dc in last st, ch 1, turn.

Row 6: Work 1 sc in first st, 1 sc in each st across, ch 2, turn, fasten off B.

Row 7: With A, work 1 dc in first st, 1 dc in each st across, ch 1, turn.

Row 8: Sk first st (dec), work 1 sc in next st, 1 sc in each st across to last 2 sts, sk st (dec), 1 sc in last st, ch 2, turn.

Rep rows 7 and 8, 10 times more—30 (32, 36) sts.

Size 6/7, last 2 rows
Row 26: Work 1 dc in first st, 1 in each st dc across, ch 1, turn.

Alternating rows of single crochet and single crochet through the back loop make up the ribbing.

Row 27: Work 1 sc in first st, sk st, * 1 sc in each of next 3 sts, sk st, rep from * 5 times, more, 1 sc in each of last 2 sts—24 sts—fasten off.

Size 8/10, last 6 rows
Row 26: Work 1 dc in first st, 1 dc in each st across, ch 1, turn.

Row 27: Work 1 sc in first st, sk st, * 1 sc in each of next 4 sts, sk st, rep from * 5 times more, 1 sc in each of last 5 sts, ch 2, turn—26 sts.

Row 28: Work 1 dc in first st, 1 dc in each st across, ch 1, turn.

Row 29: Work 1 sc in first st, 1 sc in each st across, ch 2, turn.

Row 30: Work 1 dc in first st, 1 dc in each st across, ch 1, turn.

Row 31: Work 1 sc in first st, 1 sc in each st across, fasten off.

Size 12, last 8 rows
Row 26: Work 1 dc in first st, 1 dc in each st across, ch 1, turn.

Row 27: Work 1 sc in first st, sk st, * 1 sc in each of next 4 sts, sk st, rep from * 6 times more, 1 sc in each of next 2 sts, sk st, 1 sc in last st, ch 2, turn—28 sts.

Row 28: Work 1 dc in first st, 1 dc in each st across, ch 1, turn.

Row 29: Work 1 sc in first st, 1 sc in each st across, ch 2, turn.

Row 30: Work 1 dc in first st, 1 dc in each st across, ch 1, turn.

Row 31: Work 1 sc in first st, 1 sc in each st across, ch 2, turn.

Row 32: Work 1 dc in first st, 1 dc in each st across, ch 1, turn.

Row 33: Work 1 sc in first st, 1 sc in each st across, fasten off.

Construction

1. Sew ribbing to sleeves.

2. With right sides facing, sew sleeves and side seams together.

3. Weave in loose ends, using tapestry needle. Turn right side out.

Neck Trim

Rnd 1: Join A in front left-hand corner, work 70 sc around, Sl st in first st.

Rnd 2: Sl st in next st, ch 3, work 19 dc, sk st, 14 dc, sk st, 19 dc, sk st, 13 dc, Sl st to top of ch 3.

Rnd 3: Work 1 sc in first st, 18 sc, sk st, 13 sc, sk st, 18 sc, sk st, 12 sc, Sl st to first st, fasten off.

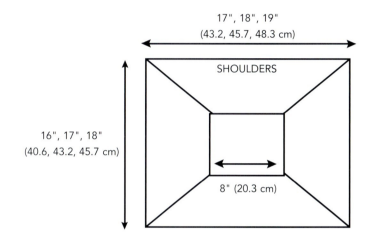

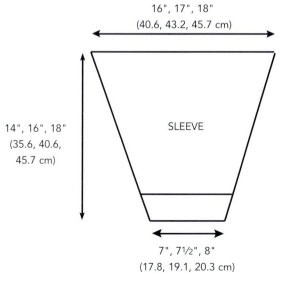

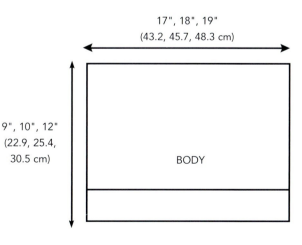

raglan crewneck sweater

design by Sharon Mann

crochet kid stuff

fingerless gloves

Keep your children's hands warm, but with the freedom to play. For skateboarding or biking or just hanging out with friends, these fingerless gloves will be a hit! They are so easy to crochet, you can make several pair in colors to match his favorite outfits.

yarn
Medium-weight smooth yarn
Shown: Wool-Ease by Lion Brand, 80% acrylic/20% wool, 3 oz (85 g)/197 yd (180 m): Rancho Red #102 (A), 1 skein; Black #153 (B), 1 skein; Grey Heather #151 (C), 1 skein

hook
6/G (4 mm)
or
8/H (5 mm)

stitches used
Single crochet
Single crochet through back loop

gauge
5 sts = 1" (2.5 cm) on 6/G hook
4 sts = 1" (2.5 cm) on 8/H hook

notions
Stitch marker
Tapestry needle

finished size
Small: 6½" (16.5 cm) cuff to top
Medium: 7¼" (18.4 cm) cuff to top

Two rows of single crochet trim the thumb opening.

Cuff

For size small, use 6/G (4 mm) hook. For size medium, use 8/H (5 mm) hook.

Foundation row: With A, ch 13. Work 1 sc in second ch from hook, 1 sc in each ch across, ch 1, turn—12 sts.

Row 1: Work 1 sc in first st, 1 sc tbl of each st across, ch 1, turn.

Rep row 1 for 22 rows more—24 rows. Using tapestry needle, sew cuff seams tog to form tube.

Palm

Worked in rnds.

Rnd 1: Join A to either side of cuff and work 24 sc evenly around, pm for beg of rnd, and cont rnds.

Rnds 2–4: Work 1 sc in each st around—24 sts.

Rnd 5: Work 2 sc in beg st, 1 sc in each of next 11 sts, 2 sc in next st, 1 sc in each of next 11 sts, change to B, ch 1, turn, fasten off A — 26 sts.

Note: To change colors, at end of row, before finishing last stitch, complete sc stitch by pulling in new color yarn through last 2 lps on hook, ch 1, turn with new color, carry previous yarn along for 6 to 8 stitches before you fasten it off.

Beg thumb opening
Row 6: Work 1 sc in first st, 1 sc in each st across, ch 1, turn.

Row 7: Work 1 sc in first st, 1 sc in each st across, change to C, ch 1, turn.

Row 8: Work 1 sc in first st, 1 sc in each st across, ch 1, turn.

Row 9: Work 1 sc in first st, 1 sc in each st across, change to B, ch 1, turn, fasten off C.

Row 10: Work 1 sc in first st, 1 sc in each st across, ch 1, turn.

Row 11: Work 1 sc in first st, 1 sc in each st across, change to A, fasten off B.

Rnd 12: Work 1 sc in next st to join rnd, 1 sc in each st around.

Rnds 13–18: Work 1 sc in each st around, Sl st in last st, fasten off.

Measure your child's hand from tip of fingers to top base of thumb. If needed, add or dec rnds bet 13 and 18.

Rnd 19: Join B, ch 1, work 1 sc in next st, change to C, 1 sc in each of next 2 sts, alternate B and C every 2 sts, ending with C, Sl st to first st, fasten off.

Thumb Opening

Rnd 1: Join A to thumb opening and work 15 sc evenly around opening.

Rnd 2: Work 1 sc in each st around, Sl st in first st, fasten off.

Weave in loose ends, using tapestry needle. Make second glove using same patt.

Accent colors are alternated every two stitches on the final row at the top of the glove.

fingerless gloves

design by Sharon Mann

crochet kid stuff

striped hoodie

Hooded sweaters are popular year-round for boys and girls. Make them in cotton yarn for spring and fall or in acrylic or wool yarn for winter. The stitch pattern gives the sweater an interesting, slightly loose texture.

yarn
Medium-weight smooth yarn
Shown: Red Heart Super Saver by Coats & Clark, 100% acrylic, 7 oz (198 g)/364 yd (333 m): Delft Blue #0313 (A), 3 skeins

Shown: Moda Dea Cartwheel by Coats & Clark, 100% wool, 1.76 oz (50 g)/77 yd (71 m): Sea Blues #9823 (B), 4 skeins

hook
9/I (5.5 mm)

stitches used
Single crochet
Single crochet through back loop
Double crochet

gauge
3 sc = 1" (2.5 cm)

notion
Tapestry needle

finished size
6/7 (8/10, 12)

Back

Beg with ribbing
Foundation row: With A, ch 9. Work 1 sc in second ch from hook, 1 sc in each ch across, ch 1, turn.

Row 1: Work 1 sc in first st, 1 sc tbl of each st across, 1 sc in last st, ch 1, turn.

Rep row 1, 54 (58, 62) times more—56 (60, 64) rows, do not fasten off.

Sweater body
Row 1: Turn ribbing horizontally, ch 1, work 56 (60, 64) sc evenly across ribbing, ch 1, turn.

Row 2: Work 1 sc in first st, * ch 1, sk st, 1 sc in next st, rep from * across, ch 1, turn.

Row 3: Work 1 sc in first st, 1 sc in next st, * ch 1, sk st, 1 sc in next sp, rep from * across, ch 1, turn.

Row 4: Rep row 2.

Row 5: Rep row 3.

Row 6: Rep row 2.

Row 7: Rep row 3.

Row 8: Work 1 sc in first st, sc across, ch 1, turn.

Row 9: Change to B, work 1 sc in first st, sc across, ch 1, turn, fasten off B.

Rep rows 2–9, 6 (7, 8) times more.

Last 2 rows: With A, work 1 sc in first st, * ch 1, sk st, 1 sc in next st, sc across, ch 1, turn. Work 1 sc in first st, sc across, fasten off.

Front

Work same as back to row 9. Foll directions for desired size.

Size 6/7
Rows 10–49: Rep rows 2–9, 5 times.

Row 50: With A, work 1 sc in first st, * ch 1, sk st, 1 sc in next st, repeat from * across, ch 1, turn.

Row 51: Work 1 sc in first st, 1 sc in next st, * ch 1, sk st, 1 sc in next sp, rep from * across, ch 1, turn.

Row 52: Work 1 sc in first st, 1 sc in next st, * ch 1, sk st, 1 sc in next sp, rep from * across, ch 1, turn.

Right shoulder
Row 53: Work 1 sc in first st, * ch 1, sk st, 1 sc in next sp, rep from * 8 times more, ch 1, sk st, 1 sc in last st, ch 1, turn.

Row 54: Sk first st, work 1 sc in next st, * ch 1, sk st, 1 sc in next sp, rep from * across, 1 sc in last st, ch 1, turn—18 sts.

Row 55: Work 1 sc in first st, * ch 1, sk st, 1 sc in next sp, rep from * 7 times more, ch 1, sk st, 1 sc in last st, ch 1, turn.

Row 56: Sk first st, work 1 sc in next st, sc across, ch 1, turn—16 sts.

Row 57: Change to B, work 1 sc in first st, sc across, ch 1, turn, fasten off A.

Row 58: With A, work 1 sc in first st, * ch 1, sk st, 1 sc in next st, rep from * across, ch 1, turn.

Row 59: Work 1 sc in first st, sc across, 1 sc in last st, fasten off.

Left shoulder
Row 53: Count in 18 sts from left side of sweater. Join A, work 1 sc in same sp, * ch 1, sk st, 1 sc in next sp, rep from * across, 1 sc in last st, ch 1, turn.

Row 54: Work 1 sc in first st, * ch 1, sk st, 1 sc in next sp, rep from * across to third to last st, ch 1, turn—16 sts.

Row 55: Work 1 sc in first st, 1 sc in next st, * ch 1, sk st, 1 sc in next sp, rep from * across, 1 sc in last st, ch 1, turn.

Row 56: Work 1 sc in first st, sc across, ch 1, turn.

Row 57: Change to B, work 1 sc in first st, sc across, ch 1, turn, fasten off B.

Row 58: With A, work 1 sc in first st, * ch 1, sk st, 1 sc in next sp, rep from * across, ch 1, turn.

Row 59: Work 1 sc in first st, sc across, 1 sc in last st, fasten off.

Size 8/10
Rows 10–57: Rep rows 2–9, 6 times.

Row 58: With A, work 1 sc in first st, * ch 1, sk st, 1 sc in next sp, rep from * across, ch 1, turn.

Row 59: Work 1 sc in first st, 1 sc in next st, * ch 1, sk st, 1 sc in next sp, rep from * across, ch 1, turn.

Row 60: Work 1 sc in first st, 1 sc in next st, * ch 1, sk st, 1 sc in next sp, rep from * across, ch 1, turn.

Right shoulder
Row 61: Work 1 sc in first st, * ch 1, sk st, 1 sc in next sp, rep from * 9 times more, ch 1, sk st, 1 sc in last st, ch 1, turn.

Row 62: Sk first st, work 1 sc in next st, * ch 1, sk st, 1 sc in next sp, rep from * across, 1 sc in last st, ch 1, turn—20 sts.

Row 63: Work 1 sc in first st, * ch 1, sk st, 1 sc in next sp, rep from * 8 times more, ch 1, sk st, 1 sc in last st, ch 1, turn.

Row 64: Sk first st, work 1 sc in next st, sc across, ch 1, turn—18 sts.

Row 65: Change to B, work 1 sc in first st, sc across, ch 1, turn, fasten off B.

Row 66: With A, work 1 sc in first st, * ch 1, sk st, 1 sc in next st, rep from * across, ch 1, turn.

Row 67: Work 1 sc in first st, sc across, 1 sc in last st, fasten off.

Left shoulder
Row 61: Count in 20 sts from left side of sweater. Join A, work 1 sc in same sp, * ch 1, sk st, 1 sc in next sp, rep from * across, 1 sc in last st, ch 1, turn.

Row 62: Work 1 sc in first st, * ch 1, sk st, 1 sc in next sp, rep from * across to third to last st, ch 1, turn.

Row 63: Work 1 sc in first st, 1 sc in next st, * ch 1, sk st, 1 sc in next sp, rep from * across, 1 sc in last st, ch 1, turn—18 sts.

Row 64: Work 1 sc in first st, sc across, ch 1, turn.

Row 65: Change to B, work 1 sc in first st, sc across, ch 1, turn, fasten off B.

Row 66: With A, work 1 sc in first st, * ch 1, sk st, 1 sc in next st, rep from * across, ch 1, turn.

Row 67: Work 1 sc in first st, sc across, 1 sc in last st, fasten off.

Size 12
Rows 10–65: Rep rows 2–9, 7 times.

Row 66: With A, work 1 sc in first st, * ch 1, sk st, 1 sc in next st, repeat from * across, ch 1, turn.

Alternating single crochet and chain spaces give the crocheted rows interesting texture. Side and underarm seam edges are trimmed with a row of single crochet in the contrast color before sewing them together.

Row 67: Work 1 sc in first st, 1 sc in next st, * ch 1, sk st, 1 sc in next sp, repeat from * across, ch 1, turn.

Row 68: Work 1 sc in first st, 1 sc in next st, * ch 1, sk st, 1 sc in next sp, rep from * across, ch 1, turn.

Right shoulder
Row 69: Work 1 sc in first st, * ch 1, sk st, 1 sc in next sp, rep from * 10 times more, ch 1, sk st, 1 sc in last st, ch 1, turn.

Row 70: Sk first st, work 1 sc in next st, * ch 1, sk st, 1 sc in next sp, rep from * across, 1 sc in last st, ch 1, turn—22 sts.

Row 71: Work 1 sc in first st, * ch 1, sk st, 1 sc in next sp, rep from * 9 times more, ch 1, sk st, 1 sc in last st, ch 1, turn.

Row 72: Sk first st, work 1 sc in next st, sc across, ch 1, turn—20 sts.

Row 73: Change to B, work 1 sc in first st, sc across, ch 1, turn, fasten off B.

Row 74: With A, work 1 sc in first st, * ch 1, sk st, 1 sc in next st, rep from * across, ch 1, turn.

Row 75: Work 1 sc in first st, sc across, 1 sc in last st, fasten off.

Left shoulder
Row 69: Count in 22 sts from left side of sweater. Join A, work 1 sc in same sp, * ch 1, sk st, 1 sc in next sp, rep from * across, 1 sc in last st, ch 1, turn.

Row 70: Work 1 sc in first st, * ch 1, sk st, 1 sc in next sp, rep from * across to third to last st, ch 1, turn.

Row 71: Work 1 sc in first st, 1 sc in next st, * ch 1, sk st, 1 sc in next sp, rep from * across, 1 sc in last st, ch 1, turn—20 sts.

Row 72: Work 1 sc in first st, sc across, ch 1, turn.

Row 73: Change to B, work 1 sc in first st, sc across, ch 1, turn, fasten off B.

Row 74: With A, work 1 sc in first st, * ch 1, sk st, 1 sc in next st, rep from * across, ch 1, turn.

Row 75: Work 1 sc in first st, sc across, sc in last st, fasten off.

Hood
Make 2.
Foundation row: With A, ch 32 (34, 36). Work 1 sc in second ch from hook, 1 sc in each ch across, ch 1, turn.

Row 1: Work 1 sc in first st, sc across, ch 1, turn.

Rows 2–3: Rep row 1.

Row 4: Work 1 sc in first st, * ch 1, sk st, 1 sc in next st, rep from * across, 1 sc in last st, ch 1, turn.

Row 5: Work 1 sc in first st, sc across, ch 1, turn.

Rep rows 4 and 5 until hood is 10" (10½", 11") [25.4 (26.9, 27.9) cm].

Sleeves
Make 2. Beg with ribbing.

Foundation row: With A, ch 9. Work 1 sc in second ch from hook, 1 sc in each ch across, ch 1, turn.

Row 1: Work 1 sc in first st, 1 sc tbl of each st across, 1 sc in last st, ch 1, turn.

Rep row 1, 20 (22, 24) times more, do not fasten off—22, (24, 26) rows.

Beg sleeve
Row 1: Turn ribbing horizontally, ch 1, work 22 (24, 26) sc evenly across ribbing, ch 1, turn.

Row 2: Work 2 sc in first st, 1 sc in each of next 4 sts, * 2 sc in next st, 1 sc in each of next 5 sts, rep from * 2 times more, 1 sc in each of next 5 sts, 2 sc in last st, ch 1, turn—27 (29, 31) sts.

Row 3: Work 1 sc in first st, * ch 1, sk st, 1 sc in next st, rep from * across, 1 sc in last st, ch 1, turn.

Row 4: Work 1 sc in first st, 1 sc in next st, * ch 1, sk st, 1 sc in next sp, rep from * across, 1 sc in last st, ch 1, turn.

Row 5: Work 1 sc in first st, * ch 1, sk st, 1 sc in next sp, rep from * across, 1 sc in last st, ch 1, turn.

Row 6: Rep row 4.

Row 7: Rep row 5.

Row 8: Rep row 4.

Row 9: Work 2 sc in first st, sc across, 2 sc in last st, ch 1, turn—29 (31, 33) sts.

Row 10: Change to B, work 1 sc in first st, sc across, ch 1, turn, fasten off B.

Row 11: With A, work 2 sc in first st, * ch 1, sk st, 1 sc in next st, rep from * across, 2 sc in last st, ch 1, turn—31 (33, 35) sts.

Row 12: Work 1 sc in first st, 1 sc in next st, * ch 1, sk st, 1 sc in next sp, rep from * across, 1 sc in last st, ch 1, turn.

Row 13: Work 1 sc in first st, * ch 1, sk st, 1 sc in next sp, rep from * across, 1 sc in last st, ch 1, turn.

Row 14: Rep row 12.

Row 15: Rep row 13.

Row 16: Rep row 12.

Row 17: Work 2 sc in first st, sc across, 2 sc in last st, ch 1, turn—33 (35, 37) sts.

Row 18: Change to B, work 1 sc in first st, sc across, ch 1, turn, fasten off B.

Row 19: With A, work 2 sc in first st, * ch 1, sk st, 1 sc in next st, rep from * across, 2 sc in last st, ch 1, turn—35 (37, 39) sts.

Size 6/7
Rows 20–43: Rep rows 12–19, 3 times more—47 sts. Fasten off A after row 23.

Row 44: Change to B, work 1 dc in first st, dc across, 1 dc in last st, fasten off.

Size 8/10
Rows 20–43: Rep rows 12–19, 3 times more—49 sts. Fasten off A after row 23.

Row 44: Work 1 sc in first st, 1 sc in next st, * ch 1, sk st, 1 sc in next sp, rep from * across, 1 sc in last st, ch 1, turn.

Row 45: Work 1 sc in first st, * ch 1, sk st, 1 sc in next sp, rep from * across, 1 sc in last st, ch 1, turn.

Row 46: Rep row 44.

Row 47: Rep row 45.

Row 48: Rep row 44.

Row 49: Work 2 sc in first st, sc across, 2 sc in last st, ch 2, turn—51 sts. Fasten off A.

Row 50: Change to B, work 1 dc in first st, dc across, 1 dc in last st, fasten off.

Size 12
Rows 20–51: Rep rows 12–19, 4 times more—53 sts.

Row 52: Work 1 sc in first st, 1 sc in next st, * ch 1, sk st, 1 sc in next, rep from * across, 1 sc in last st, ch 1, turn.

Row 53: Work 1 sc in first st, * ch 1, sk st, 1 sc in next sp, rep from * across, 1 sc in last st, ch 1, turn.

Row 54: Rep row 52.

Row 55: Rep row 53.

Row 56: Rep row 52.

Row 57: Work 2 sc in first st, sc across, 2 sc in last st, ch 2, turn—55 sts. Fasten off A.

Row 58: Change to B, work 1 dc in first st, dc across, 1 dc in last st, fasten off.

Construction
WS facing, sew front and back shoulder seams together. Turn right side out.

Neck
Row 1: Front RS facing, join B to middle of front neck opening, ch 1, 1 sc in same ch-1 sp, sc 18 (19, 20) sts evenly around right side of neck to shoulder, sc 26 (28, 30) sts around back of neck, sc 18 (19, 20) sts around left side from shoulder to beg, ch 2, turn—62 (66, 70) sts.

Row 2: Work 1 dc in first st, dc around, fasten off.

Hood
RS facing, sew top and back of hood tog. Sew hood to neck opening, RS facing, sew bottom of hood to right and left side of neck—31 (33, 35) sts on each side.

Sleeves
Fold each sleeve in half, RS facing, match center of sleeve with shoulder seam, sew each sleeve to sweater.

crochet kid stuff

Side strips

RS facing, join B, above the ribbing at right-hand cuff and sc evenly (one sc in each row) along sleeve and side of sweater, ending at top of bottom ribbing. Repeat on left sleeve and left side. RS facing, repeat on opposite side of sleeves and sides, starting above ribbing at bottom of sweater.

Finishing

WS facing, sew sleeves and sweater side seams together. Weave in loose ends. Turn right side out.

When sewing seams, lay sweater flat and match pattern of rows and strips together.

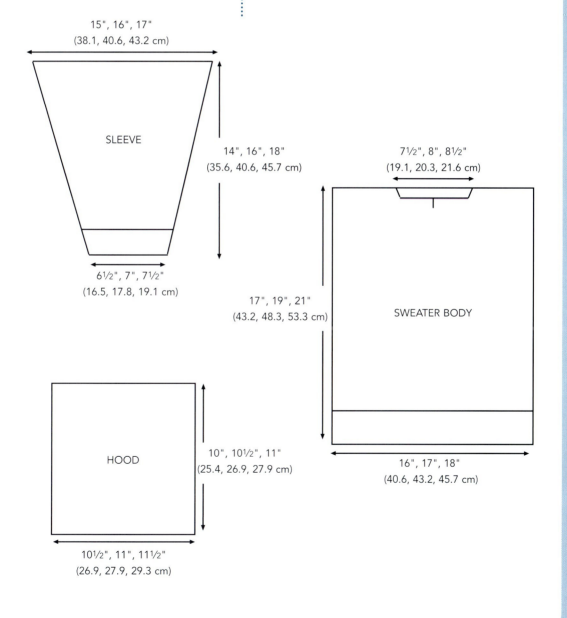

striped hoodie

design by Sharon Mann

crochet kid stuff

visor beanie

Visor beanies for kids are "in." Make the cap with stripes or a solid color, using only single crochet and double crochet stitches. Your kids will be hurrying you along to finish these popular caps. If you are fast, you can crochet one in an evening!

yarn
Medium-weight smooth yarn
Shown: Red Heart Super Saver by Coats & Clark, 100 % acrylic, 7 oz (198 g)/364 yd (333 m): Sierra Print #422 (A), 1 skein

Shown: Red Heart TLC Essentials by Coats & Clark, 100% acrylic, 6 oz (170 g): Medium Thyme #2673 (B), 1 skein

hook
8/H (5 mm)

stitches used
Single crochet
Double crochet
Front post single crochet

gauge
4 sts = 1" (2.5 cm)

notions
Stitch marker
3" × 10" (7.6 × 25.4 cm) heavy interfacing for visor
Tapestry needle

finished size
Small: 8" (20.3 cm) from crown to rim; 20" (50.8 cm) circumference
Medium: 8¼" (21 cm) from crown to rim; 21" (53.3 cm) circumference

Beanie

Worked in rnds, starting at top.

Add or reduce sc rows bet rnds 24–27 if hat length needs to be longer or shorter.

For front post single crochet, insert the hook behind the post of the stitch, rather than through the loop.

Size small
Foundation rnd: With A, ch 3, Sl st in first ch to from ring. Work 6 sc in ring, pm at beg of rnds, do not join after each rnd unless instructed to do so.

Rnd 1: Work 2 sc in each sc around—12 sc.

Rnd 2: * Work 1 sc, 2 sc in next sc, rep from * 5 times more—18 sc.

Rnd 3: * Work 2 sc, 2 sc in next sc, rep from * 5 times more—24 sc.

Rnd 4: * Work 3 sc, 2 sc in next sc, rep from * 5 times more—30 sc.

Rnd 5: * Work 4 sc, 2 sc in next sc, rep from * 5 times more—36 sc.

Rnd 6: * Work 5 sc, 2 sc in next sc, rep from * 5 times more—42 sc.

Rnd 7: * Work 6 sc, 2 sc in next sc, rep from * 5 times more—48 sc.

Rnd 8: * Work 7 sc, 2 sc in next sc, rep from * 5 times more—54 sc.

Rnd 9: * Work 8 sc, 2 sc in next sc, rep from * 5 times more—60 sc.

Rnd 10: * Work 9 sc, 2 sc in next sc, rep from * 5 times more—66 sc.

Rnd 11: * Work 10 sc, 2 sc in next sc, rep from * 5 times more—72 sc.

Rnd 12: Work 1 sc in each sc around, Sl st to first sc, fasten off A.

Rnd 13: Join B, ch 3, work 1 dc in each sc around, Sl st in top of ch 3. Fasten off B.

Rnd 14: Join A, ch 1, work 1 sc in each dc around, Sl st in first ch sp.

Rnd 15: Work 1 sc in each sc around, Sl st to first sc. Fasten off A.

Rnd 16: Join B, ch 3, work 1 dc in each sc around, Sl st in top of ch 3. Fasten off B.

Rnd 17: Join A, ch 1, work 1 sc in each dc around, Sl st in first ch sp.

Rnds 18–20: Work 1 sc in each sc around, Sl st to first sc. Fasten off A after rnd 20.

Rnd 21: Join B, ch 3, work 1 dc in each sc around, Sl st in top of ch 3. Fasten off B.

Rnd 22: Join A, ch 1, work 1 sc in each dc around, Sl st in first ch sp.

Rnds 23–25: Work 1 sc in each sc around, Sl st to first sc. Fasten off A after rnd 25.

Rnd 26: Join B, ch 3, work 1 dc in each sc around, Sl st in top of ch 3.

Rnd 27: Work 1 sc in each dc around, Sl st to first sc.

Rnd 28: Work 1 FPsc in each sc around, fasten off.

Size medium
Foll patt for size small until rnd 11 completed.

Rnd 12: * Work 11 sc, 2 sc in next sc, rep from * 3 times more—76 sc.

Rnd 13: Work 1 sc in each sc around, Sl st to first sc, fasten off A.

Rnd 14: Join B, ch 3, work 1 dc in each sc around, Sl st in top of ch 3. Fasten off B.

Rnd 15: Join A, ch 1, work 1 sc in each dc around, Sl st in first ch sp.

Rnd 16: Work 1 sc in each sc around, Sl st to first sc. Fasten off A.

Rnd 17: Join B, ch 3, work 1 dc in each sc around, Sl st in top of ch 3. Fasten off B.

Rnd 18: Join A, ch 1, work 1 sc in each dc around, Sl st in first ch sp.

Rnds 19–21: Work 1 sc in each sc around, Sl st to first sc. Fasten off A after rnd 21.

Rnd 22: Join B, ch 3, work 1 dc in each sc around, Sl st in top of ch 3. Fasten off B.

Rnd 23: Join A, ch 1, work 1 sc in each dc around, Sl st in first ch sp.

Rnds 24–26: Work 1 sc in each sc around, Sl st to first sc. Fasten off A after rnd 26.

Rnd 27: Join B, ch 3, work 1 dc in each sc around, Sl st in top of ch 3.

Rnd 28: Work 1 sc in each dc around, Sl st to first sc.

Rnd 29: Work 1 FPsc in each sc around, fasten off.

Visor
Make 2.

Foundation row: With B, ch 3. Work 1 sc in second ch from hook, 1 sc in next ch, ch 1, turn.

Row 1: Work 2 sc in first st, 1 sc in next st, ch 1, turn.

Row 2: Work 2 sc in first st, 1 sc in each of next 2 sts, ch 1, turn.

Row 3: Work 2 sc in first st, 1 sc in each of next 3 sts, ch 1, turn.

Rows 4–29: Work 1 sc in first st, sc in each st across, ch 1, turn.

Row 30: Work 1 sc in first st, 1 sc in each of next 2 sts, sk st, 1 sc in last st, ch 1, turn.

Row 31: Sk first st, work 1 sc in each of next 3 sts, ch 1, turn.

Row 32: Work 1 sc in first st, sk st, 1 sc in last st, ch 1 turn.

Row 33: Sk first st, work 1 sc in last st, fasten off.

Construction
1. Trace around visor on interfacing. Cut out ¼" (6 mm) inside the lines. Place visor pieces wrong sides together, and stitch along one edge. Insert interfacing.

2. Fold beanie in half so joining stitches of rows are on back. Pin visor in place at center front. Sew top and bottom of visor to round 27, sc row above final round 28 of cap.

3. Weave in loose ends, using tapestry needle.

Visor is sewn to second row from the bottom.

design by Sharon Mann

crochet kid stuff

polo sweater

With its zippered neck opening and a special zipper pocket on the sleeve, this sweater is sure to please. This one is made with a self-striping yarn so the color changes as you crochet. It's rugged enough to wear with jeans but dressy enough to pair with chinos.

yarn
Lightweight smooth yarn
Shown: Teseo by Di.vé, 55% wool/45% microfiber, 1.75 oz (50 g)/98 yd (90 m): #32012, 11 (12, 13) skeins

hook
9/I (5.5 mm)

stitches used
Single crochet
Single crochet through back loop
Double crochet

gauge
4 sc = 1" (2.5 cm)

notions
Tapestry needle
Two zippers, 7" (17.8 cm) long
Sewing thread to match yarn
Sewing needle

finished size
6/7 (8/10, 12)

Back

Beg with ribbing
Foundation row: Ch 9. Work 1 sc in second ch from hook, 1 sc in each ch across, ch 1, turn.

Row 1: Work 1 sc in first st, 1 sc tbl of each st across, 1 sc in last st, ch 1, turn.

Rep row 1, 52 (56, 60) times more—54 (58, 62) rows.

Cont to body
Row 1: Turn ribbing horizontally, ch 1, work 54 (58, 62) sc evenly across ribbing, ch 1, turn.

Size 6/7:
Rows 2–46: Work 1 sc in first st, 1 sc in each st across, ch 1, turn.

Row 47: * Work 1 sc in first st, 1 dc in next st, rep from * across, ch 1, turn.

Rows 48–53: Rep row 47.

Row 54: * Work 1 sc in first st, 1 dc in next st, rep from * across, ch 1, turn.

Rows 55–56: Work 1 sc in first st, 1 sc in each st across, fasten off.

Size 8/10
Rows 2–48: Work 1 sc in first st, 1 sc in each st across, ch 1, turn.

Row 49: * Work 1 sc in first st, 1 dc in next st, rep * across, ch 1, turn.

Rows 50–55: Rep row 49.

Row 56: * Work 1 sc in first st, 1 dc in next st, rep from * across, ch 1, turn.

Rows 57–58: Work 1 sc in first st, 1 sc in each st across, fasten off.

Size 12
Rows 2–50: Work 1 sc in first st, 1 sc in each st across, ch 1, turn.

Row 51: * Work 1 sc in first st, 1 dc in next st, rep from * across, ch 1, turn.

Rows 52–57: Rep row 51.

Row 58: * Work 1 sc in first st, 1 dc in next st, rep from * across, ch 1, turn.

Rows 59–60: Work 1 sc in first st, 1 sc in each st across, fasten off.

Front

Beg with ribbing
Foundation row: Ch 9. Work 1 sc in second ch from hook, 1 sc in each ch across, ch 1, turn.

Row 1: Work 1 sc in first st, 1 sc tbl of each st across, 1 sc in last st, ch 1, turn.

Rep row 1, 52 (56, 60) times more—54 (58, 62) rows.

Cont to body
Row 1: Turn ribbing horizontally, ch 1, work 54 (58, 62) sc evenly across ribbing, ch 1, turn.

Size 6/7:
Rows 2–31: Work 1 sc in first sc, 1 sc in each st across, ch 1, turn.

Right side zipper opening
Row 32: Work 1 sc in first st, 1 sc in each of next 26 sts, ch 1, turn—27 sts.

Rows 33–46: Work 1 sc in first st, 1 sc in each st across, ch 1, turn.

Rows 47–51: * Work 1 sc in first st, 1 dc in next st, rep from * across, ch 1, turn.

Rows 52–54: * Work 1 sc in first st, 1 dc in next st, rep from * across 18 sts, ch 1, turn (dec for neck opening).

Rows 55–56: Work 1 sc in first st, 1 sc in each st across, fasten off.

Left side zipper opening
Row 32: WS facing, join yarn in st next to right-side opening. Work 1 sc in first st, 1 sc in each of next 26 sts, ch 1, turn—27 sts.

Rows 33–46: Work 1 sc in first st, 1 sc in each st across, ch 1, turn.

Rows 47–51: * Work 1 sc in first st, 1 dc in next st, rep from * across, ch 1, turn.

Rows 52–54: * Work 1 sc in first st, 1 dc in next st, rep from * across 18 sts, ch 1, turn (dec for neck opening).

Rows 55–56: Work 1 sc in first st, 1 sc in each st across, fasten off.

Size 8/10
Rows 2–33: Work 1 sc in first st, 1 sc in each st across, ch 1, turn.

Right side zipper opening
Row 34: Work 1 sc in first st, 1 sc in each of next 27 sts, ch 1, turn—28 sts.

Rows 35–48: Work 1 sc in first st, 1 sc in each st across, ch 1, turn.

Rows 49–53: * Work 1 sc in first st, 1 dc in next st, rep from * across, ch 1, turn.

Rows 54–56: * Work 1 sc in first st, 1 dc in next st, rep from * across 18 sts, ch 1, turn (dec for neck opening).

Rows 57–58: Work 1 sc in first st, 1 sc in each st across, fasten off.

Left side zipper opening
Row 34: WS facing, join yarn in st next to right-side opening. Work 1 sc in first st, 1 sc in each of next 27 sts, ch 1, turn—28 sts.

Rows 35–48: Work 1 sc in first st, 1 sc in each st across, ch 1, turn.

Rows 49–53: * Work 1 sc in first st, 1 dc in next st, rep from * across, ch 1, turn.

Rows 54–56: * Work 1 sc in first st, 1 dc in next st, rep from * across 18 sts, ch 1, turn (dec for neck opening).

Rows 57–58: Work 1 sc in first st, 1 sc in each st across, fasten off.

Size 12
Rows 2–35: Work 1 sc in first st, 1 sc in each st across, ch 1, turn.

Right side zipper opening:
Row 36: Work 1 sc in first st, 1 sc in each of next 30 sts, ch 1, turn.

Rows 37–50: Work 1 sc in first st, 1 sc in each st across, ch 1, turn.

Rows 51–55: * Work 1 sc in first st, 1 dc in next st, rep from * across, ch 1, turn.

Rows 56–58: * Work 1 sc in first st, 1 dc in next st, rep from * across 20 sts, ch 1, turn (dec for neck opening).

Rows 59–60: Work 1 sc in first st, 1 sc in each st across, fasten off.

Left side zipper opening
Row 36: WS facing, join yarn in st next to right-side opening. Work 1 sc in first st, 1 sc in each of next 30 sts, ch 1, turn—31 sts.

Rows 37–50: Work 1 sc in first st, 1 sc in each st across, ch 1, turn.

Rows 51–55: * Work 1 sc in first st, 1 dc in next st, rep from * across, ch 1, turn.

Rows 56–58: * Work 1 sc in first st, 1 dc in next st, rep from * across 20 sts, ch 1, turn (dec for neck opening).

Rows 59–60: Work 1 sc in first st, 1 sc in each st across, fasten off.

Self-striping yarn in single crochet stitches make up the main body and sleeves. At the shoulders, alternating single and double crochet stitches give the fabric more texture.

RS facing, sew shoulder seams tog. Turn RS out.

Neck
Row 1: Starting at right-hand corner of neck, join yarn, ch 3, work 60 (61, 63) dc around neck evenly, ending at top of left-hand neck corner, ch 1, turn.

Row 2: Work 1 sc in each of first 2 sts, * sk st, 1 sc in each of next 2 sts, rep from * around, fasten off.

Collar
Foundation row: Ch 50 (52, 54). Work 1 sc in second ch from hook, 1 sc in each ch across, ch 1, turn.

Row 1: Work 1 sc in first st, 1 sc in each st across, ch 1, turn.

Rep row 1, 12 (12, 14) times more—16 (16, 18) rows.

RS facing, fold collar in half, sew side seams. Turn RS out.

Pin outside collar to neck and sew in place. Sew inside of collar to neck, leaving a ½" (1.3 cm) opening on both sides of inside collar to insert top tails of zipper.

Zipper closure
Pin zipper to sweater. Insert top tails of zipper in corners of inside collar. Sew sweater to front and back side of zipper for secure hold.

Right Sleeve
Beg with cuff ribbing
Foundation row: Ch 9. Work 1 sc in second ch from hook, 1 sc in each ch across, ch 1, turn.

Row 1: Work 1 sc in first st, 1 sc tbl of each st across, 1 sc in last st, ch 1, turn.

Rep row 1, 17 (19, 21) times more—19 (21, 23) rows.

Cont for sleeve
Row 1: Turn ribbing horizontally, ch 1, work 19 (21, 23) sc evenly across ribbing, ch 1, turn.

Row 2: Work 2 sc in first st, * 1 sc in each of next 4 sts, 2 sc in next st, rep from * 2 times more, sc across, 2 sc in last st, ch 1, turn—24 (26, 28) sts.

Rows 3–4: Work 1 sc in first st, sc across, ch 1, turn.

Row 5: Work 2 sc in first st, sc across, 2 sc in last st, ch 1, turn—26 (28, 30) sts.

Rows 6–7: Work 1 sc in first st, sc across, ch 1, turn.

Row 8: Work 2 sc in first st, sc across, 2 sc in last st, ch 1, turn—28 (30, 32) sts.

Rows 9–10: Work 1 sc in first st, sc across, ch 1, turn.

Row 11: Work 2 sc in first st, sc across, 2 sc in last st, ch 1, turn—30 (32, 34) sts.

Rows 12–13: Work 1 sc in first st, sc across, ch 1, turn.

Row 14: Work 2 sc in first st, sc across, 2 sc in last st, ch 1, turn—32 (34, 36) sts.

Rows 15–16: Work 1 sc in first st, sc across, ch 1, turn.

Row 17: Work 2 sc in first st, sc across, 2 sc in last st, ch 1, turn—34 (36, 38) sts.

Rows 18–19: Work 1 sc in first st, sc across, ch 1, turn.

Row 20: Work 2 sc in first st, sc across, 2 sc in last st, ch 1, turn—36 (38, 40) sts.

Rows 21–24: Work 1 sc in first st, sc across, ch 1, turn.

Row 25: Work 2 sc in first st, sc across, 2 sc in last st, ch 1, turn—38 (40, 42) sts.

Rows 26–29: Work 1 sc in first st, sc across, ch 1, turn.

Row 30: Work 2 sc in first st, sc across, 2 sc in last st, ch 1, turn—40 (42, 44) sts.

Rows 31–34: Work 1 sc in first st, sc across, ch 1, turn.

Row 35: Work 2 sc in first st, sc across, 2 sc in last st, ch 1, turn—42 (44, 46) sts.

Rows 36–39: Work 1 sc in first st, sc across, ch 1, turn.

Row 40: Work 2 sc in first st, sc across, 2 sc in last st, ch 1, turn—44 (46, 48) sts.

Row 41: Work 1 sc in first st, sc across, ch 1, turn.

Size 6/7
Row 42: * Work 1 sc in first st, 1 dc in next st, rep from * across, ch 1, turn.

Row 43: * Work 1 sc in first st, 1 dc in next st, rep from * across, fasten off.

Size 8/10:
Rows 42–44: * Work 1 sc in first st, 1 dc in next st, rep from * across, ch 1, turn.

Row 45: * Work 1 sc in first st, 1 dc in next st, rep from * across, fasten off.

Size 12:
Rows 42–46: * Work 1 sc in first st, 1 dc in next st, rep from * across, ch 1, turn.

Row 47: * Work 1 sc in first st, 1 dc in next st, rep from * across, fasten off.

Left Sleeve
Foll right sleeve patt until row 41 completed.

The upper left and right sweater fronts are worked separately to leave an opening for the zipper.

Size 6/7
Row 42: Work 1 sc in first st, 1 dc in next st, rep from * across 16 sts, ch 12, sk 12 sts, ** 1 sc in next st, 1 dc in next st, rep ** across, ch 1, turn.

Row 43: Work 1 dc in first st, 1 sc in next st, rep from * across 16 sts, 12 sc in ch sts, ** 1 sc in next st, 1 dc in next st, rep from ** across, fasten off. (Opening for sleeve zipper pocket)

Size 8/10
Row 42: Work 1 sc in first st, 1 dc in next st, rep from * across 17 sts, ch 12, sk 12 sts, ** 1 sc in next st, 1 dc in next st, rep ** across, ch 1, turn.

Row 43: Work 1 dc in first st, 1 sc in next st, rep from * across 17 sts, 12 sc in ch sts, ** 1 sc in next st, 1 dc in next st, rep from ** across, ch 2, turn. (Opening for sleeve zipper pocket)

Row 44: * Work 1 sc in first st, 1 dc in next st, rep from * across, ch 1, turn.

Row 45: * Work 1 sc in first st, 1 dc in next st, rep from * across, fasten off.

Size 12
Row 42: Work 1 sc in first st, 1 dc in next st, rep from * across 18 sts, ch 12, sk 12 sts, ** 1 sc in next st, 1 dc in next st, rep ** across, ch 1, turn.

Row 43: Work 1 dc in first st, 1 sc in next st, rep from * across 18 sts, 12 sc in ch sts, ** 1 sc in next st, 1 dc in next st, rep from ** across, ch 2, turn. (Opening for sleeve zipper pocket)

Rows 44–46: * Work 1 sc in first st, 1 dc in next st, rep from * across, ch 1, turn.

Row 47: * Work 1 sc in first st, 1 dc in next st, rep from * across, fasten off.

Sleeve Pocket

Foundation row: Ch 14. Work 1 sc in second ch from hook, 1 sc in each ch across, ch 1, turn.

Row 1: Work 1 sc in first st, 1 sc in each st across, ch 1, turn.

Rep row 1, 9 times more, fasten off.

Sleeve WS facing, sew pocket to sleeve across top of opening, sew sides and bottom of pocket to sleeve. Trim zipper to fit opening. RS facing, sew zipper to pocket opening on outside and inside of pocket for secure hold.

Construction

1. Fold each sleeve in half, RS facing, align center of sleeve with shoulder seam and sew each sleeve to sweater.
2. RS facing, sew sleeve and sweater side seams together. Turn right side out.

Long horizontal opening is made in left sleeve for zipper insertion. Patch of crocheted fabric sewn behind the zipper forms the pocket.

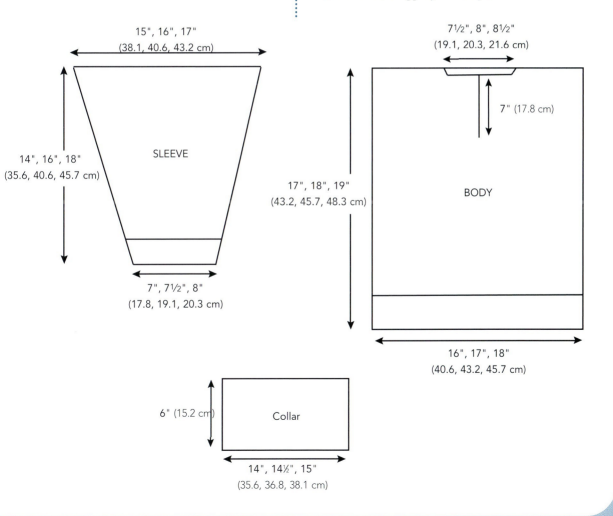

polo sweater

for fun

crochet kid stuff

for fun

design by Sharon Mann

crochet kid stuff

backpack dangles

basic pattern and add ears, noses, and google eyes to make all kinds of characters. You only need a small amount of yarn, so save your scraps from other crochet projects.

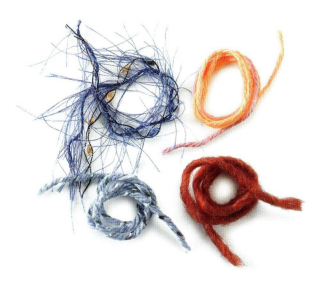

yarn
Lightweight to medium-weight yarn, any fiber
Shown: Sugar'n Cream by Lily and Cotton Pearl Thread by DMC for Cat; Red Heart Fiesta by Coats & Clark and Moda Dea Fur Ever by Coats & Clark for Button Man; Teseo by Di.vé for Monster

hook
4/E (3.5 mm)

stitch used
Single crochet

gauge
4 sc = 1" (2.5 cm)

notions
Tapestry needle
Polyester fiberfill
Sewing thread to match yarn
Sewing needle
Scraps of felt
Plastic google eyes
Beads and buttons
Glue
Jump rings
Snap hooks or lanyard hooks

finished size
3" to 5" (7.6 to 12.7 cm)

Cat

Body

Foundation rnd: Ch 4, Sl st in first ch to from ring. Do not join after each rnd.

Rnd 1: Work 6 sc in ring—6 sc.

Rnd 2: Work 2 sc in each sc—12 sc.

Rnd 3: * Work 1 sc, 2 sc in next sc, rep from * 5 times more—18 sc.

Rnd 4: * Work 2 sc, 2 sc in next sc, rep from * 5 times more—24 sc.

Rnds 5–6: Work 1 sc in each sc around.

Fasten off. Weave in loose ends, using tapestry needle. Repeat to make two pieces.

Head

Foundation rnd: Ch 4, Sl st in first ch to from ring. Do not join after each rnd.

Rnd 1: Work 6 sc in ring—6 sc.

Rnd 2: Work 2 sc in each sc—12 sc.

Rnds 3–6: Work 1 sc in each sc around.

Fasten off. Leave 10" (25.4 cm) tail to attach head to body.

Arms

Foundation rnd: Ch 5, Sl st in first ch to from ring. Do not join after each rnd.

Rnd 1: Work 8 sc in ring—8 sc.

Rnds 2–4: Work 1 sc in each sc around.

Fasten off. Leave 10" (25.4 cm) tail to attach arm to body. Repeat for other arm.

Legs

Foundation rnd: Ch 5, Sl st in first ch to from ring. Do not join after each rnd.

Rnd 1: Work 8 sc in ring—8 sc.

Rnds 2–5: Work 1 sc in each sc around.

Fasten off. Leave 10" (25.4 cm) tail to attach leg to body. Repeat for other leg.

Construction

1. Sew two body halves together, leaving a 1" (2.5 cm) opening to add fiberfill and sew closed.
2. Stuff the head, arms, and legs. Sew to body.

Finishing

1. Ch 12, fasten off. Sew to back of cat for tail.
2. Cut out two ½" (1.3 cm) felt triangles for each ear. Sew two sides of each ear together, and sew ears to top of head.
3. Cut out two small round felt cheeks, and sew them to face.
4. Glue on google eyes.
5. Sew on bead for nose.
6. Make whiskers by sewing thread beneath cheeks several times and trim to desired length.
7. Add beads and buttons for decoration.
8. Attach jump ring to top of head, and attach snap hook or lanyard hook for hanging.

Google eyes, a bead nose, and thread whiskers give the cat dangle personality.

Button Man

Crochet body and head, following directions for cat.

1. Sew on strings of buttons for arms and legs.
2. Crochet chain of fur yarn to make fur collar.
3. Glue on google eyes.
4. Add beads and buttons for decoration.
5. Attach jump ring to top of head, and attach snap hook or lanyard hook for hanging.

Monster

Crochet body, following directions for cat.

1. Sew two halves together, leaving 2¼" (5.7 cm) opening for mouth.
2. Cut out 2" (5.1 cm) circle of black felt. Fold felt circle in half and insert in opening. Sew top half of felt circle to mouth opening. Stuff body and sew bottom half of felt circle to mouth opening.
3. Sew on white beads for teeth.
4. Glue on google eyes.
5. Attach jump ring to top of head, and attach snap hook or lanyard hook for hanging.

Strings of assorted buttons form this dangle's arms and legs.

White beads give the monster dangle his bite.

design by Sharon Mann

crochet kid stuff

fun and crazy pencil toppers

Pencil toppers will make your kids laugh out loud. Let your creativity soar. Make them with any type of yarn and use lots of beads, buttons, felt, and fancy threads. Most likely you'll have all the supplies you need in your sewing basket and yarn baskets.

yarn
Cotton pearl threads
Metallic braid threads
Novelty yarns, such as fur yarn and jelly yarn

hooks
1/B (2.25 mm)
2/C (2.75 mm)
4/E (3.5 mm)

stitch used
Single crochet

gauge
Varies

notions
Graphite pencils
Tapestry needle
Sewing thread to match yarn colors
Sewing needle
Felt scraps
Glue
Plastic google eyes
Beading needle
Seed and medium-size beads
Small and medium-size buttons
Small amount of polyester fiberfill

finished size
Fits standard pencil

Take a closer look at the Santa, dinosaur, and pumpkin pencil toppers.

Basic Pattern

Use 1/B (2.25 mm) or 2/C (2.75 mm) hook with double strand of cotton pearl thread.

Use 4/E (3.5 mm) hook with single strand or novelty yarn.

Foundation row: Ch 13. Work 1 sc in second ch from hook, 1 sc in each ch across, ch 1, turn.

Row 1: Work 1 sc in first st, 1 sc in each st across, ch 1, turn.

Rep row 1 until piece wraps around pencil and edges just meet, fasten off. Weave in loose ends, using tapestry needle.

Santa

Body

Using double strand of red #5 cotton pearl thread and 1/B (2.25 mm) hook, foll basic patt for body.

Beard and Hair

Make 2.
Use 1/B hook and single strand of white #5 pearl thread for beard.

Foundation row: Ch 8. Work 1 sc in second ch from hook, 1 sc in each ch across, ch 1, turn.

Row 1: Work 1 sc in first st, 1 sc in each st across, ch 1, turn.

Row 2: * Ch 3, work 1 sc in next st, rep from * across, fasten off.

Construction
1. Using matching sewing thread, sew side and top of pencil topper.

2. Cut out ½" (1.3 cm) circle of pink felt for the face, and sew to pencil topper.

3. Glue on eyes, and sew on red bead for nose.

4. Sew on hair around top of pencil. Sew beard halfway down on face.

5. Cut out 1¼" (3.2 cm) circle of red felt for hat. Cut circle in half. Fold half circle into cone and stitch together. Sew to top of pencil topper. Cut out ¼" × 2" (6 mm × 5.1 cm) piece of white felt. Wrap around base of hat. Trim excess and glue or stitch to hat.

6. Cut out ¼" × 1½" (6 mm × 3.8 cm) piece of black felt for belt. Glue around Santa's waist, and sew button on front of belt.

7. Stitch beads to bottom of Santa, alternating red and white.

Dinosaur
Using double strand of green #5 cotton pearl thread and 1/B (2.25 mm) hook, foll basic patt for body.

Nose
Use single strand of green #5 cotton pearl thread and 1/B hook for nose.

Foundation rnd: Ch 4, Sl st to form ring.

Rnd 1: Work 6 sc in ring.

Rnd 2: Work 1 sc in each st around, Sl st in beg st, fasten off.

Construction
1. Using matching sewing thread, sew side and top of pencil topper.

2. Sew nose to pencil topper.

3. Cut two pieces of felt ½" (1.3 cm) wide by length of dinosaur from top of head to bottom. Layer pieces and notch points along one edge. Sew pieces together; then sew to head and back of dinosaur for scales. Sew seed beads along points of scales.

4. Glue on plastic google eyes, and sew on beads for mouth.

5. Weave metallic thread in and out of sc around body.

Pumpkin
Using double strand of orange #5 cotton pearl thread and 1/B (2.25 mm) hook, foll basic patt for body, but ch 17 to start.

fun and crazy pencil toppers

Construction

1. Using matching sewing thread, sew side and top of pencil topper.

2. Stuff head with small amount of fiberfill. Weave piece of metallic thread around neck, ½" (1.3 cm) down from top of head, pull tight. Tie in bow and sew on green bead.

3. Sew two green beads on top of head for stem.

4. Cut out small triangles of black felt for nose and mouth; glue in place. Glue on plastic google eyes.

5. Sew three small buttons on front of pumpkin pencil topper.

Cat

Using double strand of purple #5 cotton pearl thread and 1/B (2.25 mm) hook, foll basic patt for body.

Construction

1. Using matching sewing thread, sew side and top of pencil topper.

2. Sew two sc stitches together at top of head to accentuate pointed ears.

3. Embroider nose with pink thread. Thread yarn under nose several times for whiskers or weave short pieces of jelly yarn under nose. Trim to desired length. 4. Glue on google eyes.

5. Ch 12 for tail. Sew tail to back bottom of pencil topper. Sew on beads around bottom of body.

Firecracker

Using one strand each of red and white #5 cotton pearl thread and 1/B (2.25 mm) hook, foll basic patt for body.

Construction

1. Using matching sewing thread, sew side and top of pencil topper.

2. Sew rows of red and blue beads up sides of topper and sew beads to top.

3. Fringe bottom with blue pearl thread.

Fuzzy Wuzzy

Using single strand of fur yarn and 4/E (3.5 mm) hook, foll basic patt for body.

Construction

1. Using matching sewing thread, sew side and top of pencil topper.

2. Glue on google eyes.

Jelly Topper

Using single strand of jelly yarn and 4/E (3.5 mm) hook, foll basic patt for body.

Construction

1. Using matching sewing thread, sew side and top of pencil topper.

2. Glue on google eyes.

3. Cut six pieces of jelly yarn, each 3½" (8.9 cm) long. Thread pieces through top of pencil topper, fold in half, and wrap small piece of felt around strands to hold them in place. Glue ends of felt together.

4. Sew beads around felt.

Take a closer look at the cat, firecracker, fuzzy wuzzy, and jelly topper.

fun and crazy pencil toppers

design by Sharon Mann

crochet kid stuff

small change pouches

These pouches zip shut, so they can be used to carry lunch money, keys, or whatever little tokens they wish. Personalize them with buttons or beads.

Pouch

Foundation row: Ch 17. Work 1 sc in second ch from hook, 1 sc in each ch across, ch 1, turn.
Row 1: Work 1 sc in first st, 1 sc in each st across, ch 1, turn.
Rows 2–16: Rep row 1.
Sc evenly around outside of coin purse, fasten off.

Construction

1. Fold piece vertically. Sew up each side and ½" (1.3 cm) into top on each side. Trim zipper to fit opening. Hand sew zipper in place.

2. Sew on beads and buttons for decoration.

3. Attach jump ring to top of football and attach snap hook or lanyard hook for hanging.

---

yarn
Lightweight smooth yarn
Shown: Sierra by Cascade, 80% cotton/20% wool, 3.5 oz (100 g)/ 191 yd (176 m): Brown #41 or Turquoise #60, 1 skein

hook
4/E (3.5 mm)

stitch used
Single crochet

gauge
4 sc = 1" (2.5 cm)

notions
Tapestry needle
Sewing thread to match yarn
Sewing needle
Zipper, 7" (17.8 cm) long
Beads and buttons
Jump ring
Snap hook or lanyard hook

finished size
2½" × 4" (6.4 × 10.2 cm)

design by Sharon Mann

crochet kid stuff

hacky sacks

Hacky sacks are great for building coordination. Kids love to kick them back and forth with friends or by themselves. Crochet them in bright colors—stuff them with plastic craft pellets or small dried mung beans.

Hacky Sack

Make 2 halves. Worked in rnds, starting at top and bottom.

Foundation rnd: With A, ch 4, Sl st in first ch to form ring. Work 6 sc in ring, pm at beg of rnds, do not join after each rnd unless instructed to do so.

Rnd 1: Work 2 sc in each sc—12 sc.

Rnd 2: * Work 1 sc, 2 sc in next sc, rep from * 5 times more—18 sc.

Rnd 3: * Work 2 sc, 2 sc in next sc, rep from * 5 times more—24 sc.

Rnd 4: * Work 3 sc, 2 sc in next sc, rep from * 5 times more—30 sc.

Rnd 5: * Work 4 sc, 2 sc in next sc, rep from * 5 times more—36 sc.

Rnd 6: * Work 5 sc, 2 sc in next sc, rep from * 5 times more—42 sc.

Rnds 7–9: Work 1 sc in each sc around.

Rnd 10: Work 1 sc in each sc around, change to B (stripe).

Rnds 11–12: Work 1 sc in each sc around, fasten off.

Rep for second half, starting with B and changing to A for stripe.

Finishing

1. Weave in loose ends, using tapestry needle.

2. Measure approximately ⅓ cup of plastic pellets or beans and place in center of 8" (20.3 cm) square of plastic wrap. Gather plastic wrap to make ball, trim excess, and tape closed. Place ball into one hacky sack half. Place other hacky sack half on top. The ball should be filled, but not packed tight. Sew two halves together.

yarn
Cotton crochet thread, size 10
Shown: Aunt Lydia's Double Strand by Coats & Clark, 100% cotton, 300 yd (274 m): Parakeet/Dark Royal #457 (A), 1 ball; Victory Red/Mexicana #443 (B), 1 ball

hook
1/B (2.25 mm)

stitch used
Single crochet

gauge
6 sc 1" (2.5 cm)

notions
Stitch marker
Tapestry needle
One bag plastic stuffing pellets or dried mung beans
Plastic wrap

finished size
6½" (16.5 cm) circumference

crochet kid stuff

snuggle-up blanket

Let your kids choose their favorite colors. Using a double strand of yarn (one multicolor and one solid) and a large hook, you'll have this loving gift done in no time at all. Single crochet in the back loop of each stitch gives the blanket a ribbed texture.

Blanket
Use double strand throughout: one strand self-striping yarn and one strand solid color.

Foundation row: With one strand each of B and D, ch 78. Work 1 sc in second ch from hook, 1 sc in each ch across, ch 1, turn.

Row 1: Work 1 sc in first st, 1 sc tbl of each st across, 1 sc in last st, ch 1, turn.

Rep row 1 until blanket is 32" (81.3 cm) or desired width. Change solid color every four rows, using sequence: B, A, C, A.

Fasten off. Weave in loose ends, using tapestry needle.

Fringe
Cut 60 pieces of each solid-color yarn, each 12" (30.5 cm) long. Combine one strand of each color. At end of every other row, attach fringe in Larks Head Knot (fold yarn in half, pull lp through sp, bring ends of yarn through lp, pull tight). Trim fringe to desired length.

yarn
Medium-weight acrylic yarn in three solid colors
Shown: Red Heart Super Saver by Coats & Clark, 100% acrylic, 7 oz (198 g)/364 yd (333 m): Aran #0313 (A), 1 skein; Royal #0385 (B), 1 skein; Burgundy #0376 (C), 1 skein

Lightweight, self-striping, acrylic yarn
Shown: Moda Dea Sassy Stripes by Coats & Clark, 100% acrylic, 1.76 oz (50 g)/147 yd (135 m): Lucky #6997 (D), 4 skeins

hook
P (11.5 mm)

stitches used
Single crochet
Single crochet through back loop

gauge
2 sc = 1" (2.5 cm)

notion
Tapestry needle

finished size
32" × 46" (81.3 × 116.8 cm)

Slip Knot and Chain

All crochet begins with a chain, into which is worked the foundation row for your piece. To make a chain, start with a slip knot. To make a slip knot, make a loop several inches from the end of the yarn, insert the hook through the loop, and catch the tail with the end (1).

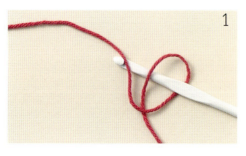

Draw the yarn through the loop on the hook (2).

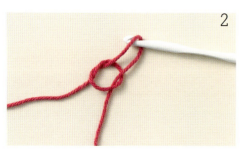

After the slip knot, start your chain. Wrap the yarn over the hook (yarn over) and catch it with the hook. Draw the yarn through the loop on the hook. You have now made 1 chain. Repeat the process to make a row of chains. When counting chains, do not count the slip knot at the beginning or the loop that is on the hook (3).

Slip Stitch

The slip stitch is a very short stitch, which is mainly used to join 2 pieces of crochet together when working in rounds. To make a slip stitch, insert the hook into the specified stitch, wrap the yarn over the hook (1),

and then draw the yarn through the stitch and the loop already on the hook (2).

Single Crochet

Insert the hook into the specified stitch, wrap the yarn over the hook, and draw the yarn through the stitch so there are 2 loops on the hook (1).

Wrap the yarn over the hook again and draw the yarn through both loops (2).

When working in single crochet, always insert the hook through both top loops of the next stitch, unless the directions specify front loop or back loop only.

Single Crochet 2 Stitches Together

This decreases the number of stitches in a row or round by 1. Insert the hook into the specified stitch, wrap the yarn over the hook, and draw the yarn through the stitch so there are 2 loops on the hook (1).

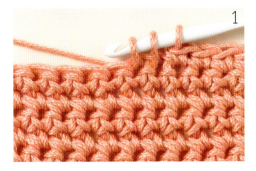

Insert the hook through the next stitch, wrap the yarn over the hook, and draw the yarn through the stitch so there are 3 loops on the hook (2).

Wrap the yarn over the hook again and draw the yarn through all the loops at once.

Single Crochet Through the Back Loop

This creates a distinct ridge on the side facing you. Insert the hook through the back loop only of each stitch, rather than under both loops of the stitch. Complete the single crochet as usual.

crochet stitches

Double Crochet

Wrap the yarn over the hook, insert the hook into the specified stitch, and wrap the yarn over the hook again. Draw the yarn through the stitch so there are 3 loops on the hook (1).

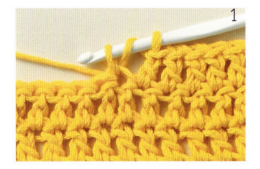

Wrap the yarn over the hook again and draw it through 2 of the loops so there are now 2 loops on the hook (2).

Wrap the yarn over the hook again and draw it through the last 2 loops (3).

Double Crochet Two Stitches Together

This decreases the number of stitches in a row or round by 1. Wrap the yarn over the hook, insert the hook into the specified stitch, and wrap the yarn over the hook again. Draw the yarn through the stitch so there are 3 loops on the hook. Wrap the yarn over the hook again and draw it through 2 of the loops so there are now 2 loops on the hook. Wrap the yarn over the hook and pick up a loop in the next stitch, so there are now 4 loops on the hook. Wrap the yarn over the hook and draw through 2 loops, yarn over and draw through 3 loops to complete the stitch.

Triple, or Treble, Crochet

Wrap the yarn over the hook twice, insert the hook into the specified stitch, and wrap the yarn over the hook again. Draw the yarn through the stitch so there are 4 loops on the hook. Wrap the yarn over the hook again (1)

and draw it through 2 of the loops so there are now 3 loops on the hook (2).

Wrap the yarn over the hook again and draw it through 2 of the loops so there are now 2 loops on the hook (3).

Wrap the yarn over the hook again and draw it through the last 2 loops (4).

abbreviations

approx	approximately		patt	pattern
beg	begin/beginning		pc	popcorn
bet	between		pm	place marker
BL	back loop(s)		prev	previous
BP	back post		rem	remain/remaining
BPdc	back post double crochet		rep	repeat(s)
CC	contrasting color		rev sc	reverse single crochet
ch	chain		rnd(s)	round(s)
ch-	refers to chain or space previously made, e.g., ch-1 space		RS	right side(s)
			sc	single crochet
ch lp	chain loop		sc2tog	single crochet 2 stitches together
ch-sp	chain space		sk	skip
CL	cluster(s)		Sl st	slip stitch
cm	centimeter(s)		sp(s)	space(s)
cont	continue		st(s)	stitch(es)
dc	double crochet		tch	turning chain
dc2tog	double crochet 2 stitches together		tbl	through back loop(s)
			tfl	through front loop(s)
dec	decrease/decreases/decreasing		tog	together
			tr	triple crochet
FL	front loop(s)		tr2tog	triple crochet 2 stitches together
foll	follow/follows/following		WS	wrong side(s)
FP	front post		yd	yard(s)
FPsc	front post single crochet		yo	yarn over
FPtr	front post triple crochet		yoh	yarn over hook
g	gram(s)		[ ]	Work instructions within brackets as many times as directed
hdc	half double crochet			
inc	increase/increases/increasing		*	Repeat instructions following the single asterisk as directed
lp(s)	loop(s)			
m	meter(s)		**	Repeat instructions between asterisks as many times as directed or repeat from a given set of instructions
MC	main color			
mm	millimeter(s)			
oz	ounce(s)			
p	picot			

crochet for kids